Race and the War on Poverty

Race and Culture in the American West
Quintard Taylor, Series Editor

Race and the War on Poverty

From Watts to East L.A.

ROBERT BAUMAN

UNIVERSITY OF OKLAHOMA PRESS : NORMAN

Library of Congress Cataloging-in-Publication Data

Bauman, Robert, 1964–
Race and the war on poverty : from Watts to East L.A. / Robert Bauman.
p. cm. — (Race and culture in the American West ; v. 3)
Includes bibliographical references and index.
ISBN 978-0-8061-3965-4 (hardcover : alk. paper) 1. Economic assistance,
Domestic—California—Los Angeles—History—20th century. 2. Poverty—Social
aspects—California—Los Angeles—History—20th century. 3. Los Angeles
(Calif.)—Economic conditions—20th century. 4. Los Angeles (Calif.)—Race
relations—History—20th century. I. Title.
HC108.L55B38 2008
362.5′5608900979494—dc22
2008015852

Race and the War on Poverty: From Watts to East L.A. is Volume 3 in the Race
and Culture in the American West series.

Copyright © 2008 by the University of Oklahoma Press, Norman, Publishing
Division of the University. Manufactured in the U.S.A.

1 2 3 4 5 6 7 8 9 10

For Stephanie,
who opened my mind to possibilities,
my eyes to the world around me,
and my heart to love

Contents

Illustrations

Acknowledgments

THIS BOOK HAS TAKEN SO long to write that it is hard to know where to begin, but since the idea for it originated in a graduate seminar at the University of California, Santa Barbara, I will start there. For their support during my time at UCSB, I would like to thank Laura Kalman, Randy Bergstrom, Otis Graham, Mary Furner, and Richard Flacks. All of you made signal contributions to what was then a dissertation, and I thank you for your advice and support.

This book is significantly different from, and I think and hope better than, the dissertation, and I have a number of people to thank for that. First, to Marc Rodriguez, thank you for reviving my academic career. Somehow you found me and invited me to participate in the War on Poverty conference you and Annelise Orleck organized at Princeton University in 2003. It is not an overstatement to say that that meeting of minds reignited my passion for this topic and influenced me to approach it very differently than I had in my dissertation. I have no doubt that without the conference, this book would not have happened. So to all of the conference participants, especially Marc and Annelise, but also Michael Katz, Christina Greene, Rhonda Williams, Tom Kiffmeyer, Karen Tani, and William Clayson, thank you for sharing your research, knowledge, and insights into the War on Poverty.

Parts of this book were published in an article in the January 2007 issue of the *Journal of Urban History*. I would like to thank the journal editor, David Goldfield, for inviting me to submit my work for publication in that journal. I would also like to thank the anonymous reviewers for the journal, who made most useful suggestions for the completion of my article as well as this book.

A paper I presented at the American Historical Association led directly to the *Journal of Urban History* article and to this book. I would like to thank all the participants on that panel, particularly Marc Rodriguez and Alice O'Connor, for their careful readings of my work, their insightful comments, and their support of this project. Quintard Taylor's presence at the panel eventually led to my book contract with the University of Oklahoma Press, so a special thank-you to Quintard for thinking this work was worthy of publication in the series. At the University of Oklahoma Press, I would also like to thank Chuck Rankin, Jay Dew, Sarah Nestor, and, particularly, my editor, Matt Bokovoy.

One last conference played a significant role in focusing my thinking on a few key issues in this book. The conference "The War on Poverty and Grassroots Struggles for Racial and Economic Justice," held at the Miller Center for Public Affairs at the University of Virginia in November 2007, brought together some of the brightest minds and leading scholars of the War on Poverty. It was there that I first used the term "long war on poverty" during some of our group discussions. The conference was truly the most intellectually stimulating and enjoyable couple of days I can remember. For that, I would like to thank the conference organizers, Guian McKee and Lisa Hazirjian, as well as all of the participants, particularly Annelise Orleck, Marc Rodriguez, Rhonda Williams, Tom Kiffmeyer, William Clayson, Laurie Green, Dan Cobb, Kent Germany, Amy Jordan, Irene Holliman, Wesley Phelps, Susan Ashmore, and Tom Jackson, with each of whom I enjoyed enlightening conversations. I was humbled and honored to be part of such a stellar group of scholars.

Research for the project took me to a number of archival collections over a period of years. At each of the collections, I found the archivists and librarians (some of whom have since moved on to other endeavors) superbly helpful and professional. I would specifically like to thank: Hynda Rudd, Rob Freeman, and the staff at the Los Angeles City Archives; Sarah Cooper and Mary Tyler of the Southern California Library for Social Studies and Research; Linda Hanson of the Lyndon Baines Johnson Presidential Library; Claude Zachary of the California Social Welfare Archives at the University of Southern California; David Sigler at the Special Collections Library at California State University, Los Angeles; Tony Lewis at the Special Collections Library at the University of California, Santa Barbara; and the staff of the Special Collections Library and the Chicano Studies Research Center at UCLA.

Over the years, I have received a number of grants to help offset the costs of research. Among them were a Lyndon Baines Johnson Presidential Library Research Grant, a Historical Society of Southern California/Haynes Foundation Research Grant, and an Edward R. Meyer Project Award from the College of Liberal Arts at Washington State University. I owe a sincere debt of gratitude to each of those institutions for making my research and the completion of this book possible.

At my home campus, Washington State University, Tri-Cities, I have one history colleague, Brigit Farley. Brigit has been amazingly generous and supportive from the beginning of my employment at WSU. My departmental colleagues in Vancouver and Pullman, particularly former chair Roger Schlesinger and current cochairs John Kicza and Ray Sun, have also offered kind words and encouragement over the years.

My family has been especially supportive throughout this lengthy process. To my parents, Betty and Bert Enserink, and my wife's parents, Ben and Rosie San Miguel, a special thanks for their generous support and their hospitality during my research trips to Southern California. It is nice when you can go "home" to do research.

Most of all, I must thank my wife, Stephanie, and my children, Robert and Rachel. To my children (neither of whom was born when I began this project), thank you for making this take longer than it should have. Bike rides, living-room dances, and backyard whiffle-ball games were much more fun than writing; they helped keep me centered and reminded me what is most important in life. I have been working on this book off and on through much of my seventeen-year marriage to Stephanie. She has read a good portion of various versions of the manuscript during this lengthy period, even though she has an academic career of her own, and she has offered unwavering support and encouragement and, most of all, her boundless love. It is to her that I dedicate this book.

Race and the War on Poverty

Introduction

IN DECEMBER 2001 A PARTY is held in Los Angeles—a party attended by local, state, and national dignitaries and celebrities. The celebration honors Gloria Molina. The daughter of a Mexican mother and a Mexican American father, Molina grew up in the largely Mexican American community of Pico Rivera, east of downtown Los Angeles. The festive occasion commemorates Molina's twenty years of public service. Her political career is, indeed, significant, for she was the first Latina elected to the State of California Assembly, the first elected to the Los Angeles City Council, and the first elected to the Los Angeles County Board of Supervisors.[1]

Four years later, in August 2005, a different sort of celebration occurs in another community in Los Angeles. Thousands of spectators, mostly African Americans but many Latinos as well, ignore the heat and line the streets of South Central Los Angeles to attend the Watts Summer Festival. Long a community tradition, this year's festival garners special attention and takes on additional significance as it commemorates forty years since the Watts riots of 1965.[2]

About ten miles from Watts, just off the Interstate 5 freeway in the city of Commerce, the forty-six-acre TELACU Industrial Park figures prominently in the urban landscape. Formerly the B. F. Goodrich tire factory, the Spanish Colonial Revival exterior of the park's main building features a giant, colorful mural, *The Pride of Our Heritage* or *El Orgullo de Nuestra Herencia,* depicting Mexican American contributions to history. The mural undoubtedly catches the eyes of travelers stuck in Los Angeles's unrelenting traffic.[3]

Gloria Molina's political career, the Watts Summer Festival parade, and the TELACU Industrial Park: three thriving political, cultural, and economic institutions in Los Angeles. And all three developed as a result of the War on Poverty in that city. All three represent the myriad ways that African Americans, Chicanos, and Chicanas in Los Angeles connected the War on Poverty to movements for economic, cultural, and political empowerment. In addition, all three signify distinct developments in African Americans' and Mexican Americans' fight to define their freedom and challenge racial boundaries in the evolving city of Los Angeles.

"This administration today, here and now, declares unconditional war on poverty in America," President Lyndon Johnson proclaimed to the nation in his "State of the Union" address on January 8, 1964.[4] Two months later, on March 16, Johnson presented a "Message on Poverty," in which he called for a "national war on poverty."[5] On August 20 of the same year, the president signed the Economic Opportunity Act, which provided both the strategy and the ammunition to fight the War on Poverty. The act allowed local communities to establish Community Action Agencies (CAAs), which could apply to the newly created Office of Economic Opportunity (OEO) for federal funds to support the development of service programs for their communities. The administration hoped the act would "strengthen, supplement, and coordinate efforts" to "eliminate the paradox of poverty in the midst of plenty."[6]

One year later, much of South Central Los Angeles burned as the African American community erupted in violence. Thousands of miles away, President Johnson brooded at his ranch in Texas, wondering why the landmark pieces of legislation he had signed—the Civil Rights Act of 1964, the Voting Rights Act of 1965 (signed just days prior to the violence in Watts), and the Economic Opportunity Act—had not alleviated the problems blacks faced in Los Angeles and prevented urban unrest.[7] This book explores the threads that wove together the War on Poverty, the Watts revolt, and movements for economic, cultural, and political empowerment in multiracial Los Angeles in the 1960s.

As part of the American West, Los Angeles has been more racially diverse from its inception than cities in other regions of the country. Indeed, Richard White has argued that it is the region's unique history of race relations and its multiracial population, from early in its history, that gives the American West its true distinctiveness. That is certainly true of Los Angeles.[8] In fact, the initial founders of El Pueblo de Nuestra Señora la Reina de Los Angeles de Porciúncula in 1781 were of Mexican and/or African descent.[9] Thus, multiracialism always has been a significant part of the social fabric of Los Angeles.[10]

The federal government's War on Poverty in the 1960s added to and altered some of the permutations of race in the city. Indeed, race and racial politics acted as both a stimulus and a hindrance to the War on Poverty in Los Angeles. Some scholars, most notably Frances Fox Piven and Richard Cloward, focused on the origins of the War on Poverty, arguing that the social unrest of the civil rights movement led directly to the War on Poverty.[11] This book argues that the War on Poverty intersected with a multifaceted and evolving collection of movements for cultural, political, and economic empowerment in Los Angeles during the implementation of the policy. Gareth Davies, in his *From Opportunity to Entitlement,* also notes the connection between the implementation of the War on Poverty and the civil rights movement, but his work is focused more on the shift from opportunity to entitlement in federal policy.[12]

By looking at implementation, scholars can explore the experiences of ordinary people within a community context. Some have begun to examine the implementation of other periods of social policy. Thomas Krainz, for instance, deftly explores the implementation of Progressive era welfare programs in Colorado. In addition some scholars, such as Annelise Orleck, Nancy Naples, and Christina Greene, have studied the implementation of War on Poverty programs in particular communities. Their approach seems especially relevant in studying the War on Poverty, since it was created to include "maximum feasible participation" of the poor in local communities. This study, then, looks at the ways in which local neighborhoods and communities in Los Angeles implemented their own versions of the War on Poverty.[13]

Davies, Orleck, Greene, Jill Quadagno, and Judith Russell all emphasize race in their treatments of the War on Poverty, but their discussions of race are biracial (black and white), not multiracial, whereas this book is a multiracial history of the War on Poverty in Los Angeles.[14] I explore the history of race in the city through the creation and development of four distinct CAAs initiated as part of the War on Poverty in Los Angeles. Those four agencies include one "official" one (controlled by local governments) and three "unofficial" ones (controlled by organizations of ordinary citizens). The official agency, the Economic and Youth Opportunities Agency (EYOA), eventually collapsed under the weight of political turf battles, tenacious intransigence by city officials, strategic and ideological differences among black leaders and civil rights activists, and volatile tensions and divisions between blacks and Latinos.

In response to the failure of the EYOA, African Americans and Latinos, encouraged by the culturally nationalist ethos of the black power and Chicano movements and supported and aided by labor unions, established separate War on Poverty organizations outside the domain of the "official" War on Poverty agency under Los Angeles city and county control.[15] African Americans in Watts created the Watts Labor Community Action Committee (WLCAC), while Mexican Americans in East Los Angeles formed the East Los Angeles Community Union (TELACU). Indeed, these ethnically distinct "community unions" provided services and a sense of racial/ethnic/cultural pride and solidarity for Latino and African American neighborhoods and communities in Los Angeles in "spaces of meaning" to the residents of those neighborhoods and communities.[16]

Chicana activists in East Los Angeles founded the fourth organization I have included in this study of race and the War on Poverty in the city. Scholars such as Orleck, Greene, and Naples have used gender in addition to race in their examinations of the implementation of the War on Poverty; it is my intent to further demonstrate the centrality of gender and women's community organizations nationally through a study of the Chicana Service Action Center (CSAC). The CSAC, created by the Chicana feminist organization Comisión Femenil Mexicana Nacional in 1972, incorporated the culturally nationalistic ideals of the Chicano movement, along with feminist ideology, into an antipoverty agency. Its goals of bringing War on Poverty services and programs to needy women in East Los Angeles, as well as training women to become leaders in the Mexican American community, demonstrated the malleability of the War on Poverty and its intricate relationship with movements for cultural, economic, political, and gender empowerment. Indeed, the War on Poverty challenged the traditional racial and gendered power relationships in Los Angeles. Or, perhaps more accurately, ordinary people in the WLCAC, TELACU, and CSAC used the framework, ideals, and programs of the War on Poverty—as well as the burgeoning ideologies of black power, brown power, and feminism—to challenge traditional racial and gendered power relationships in Los Angeles.

Importantly, these antipoverty organizations were all created by culturally nationalistic groups intent on improving the lives of poor people *in their own communities*.[17] These agencies contained a clear, unmistakable geographical component. Even the names of the organizations, the Watts Labor Community Action Committee and The East Los Angeles Community Union, define the geographical boundaries of their work. Located in communities only ten miles apart and supported by some of the same labor unions, the WLCAC and TELACU nonetheless fought their battles against poverty and pursued the shared goals of cultural and economic empowerment separately from each other. Only the CSAC crossed its initial geographical boundaries in the 1970s, establishing additional antipoverty centers for women in other sections of Los Angeles. Those centers, though, were in largely Chicano neighborhoods, and so the CSAC, true to its name as well, remained a Chicana organization. Thus, the War on Poverty in Los Angeles was fought in racially and ethnically distinct neighborhoods rather than as an interracial movement of the poor.

It was fought in that way because ordinary people used it as part of the ongoing struggle to define their economic, cultural, and political freedom. African Americans and Mexican Americans in Los Angeles shared a similar, yet distinct, past. Both groups had battled racially restrictive covenants, segregated schools, redlining practices, and a lack of access to jobs, transportation, and health care throughout their histories in Los Angeles. Yet they had unique experiences as well—different timing of migrations, distinct religious affiliations, and geographically distinct centers of populations among them. For both groups, the War on Poverty created an opportunity to use those experiences and the evolving ideologies of the civil rights movements in their communities to continue their fight for the expansion of their freedom and of American democracy.

This story, then, does not concern whether the War on Poverty succeeded or failed at eliminating poverty; other scholars have thoroughly debated that aspect of the story.[18] Instead, it describes how the War on Poverty evolved in a myriad of ways in Los Angeles and how, through that evolution, it influenced movements for political, cultural, and economic empowerment. Those same movements—the black freedom, Chicano, and feminist movements—in turn shaped the War on Poverty in Los Angeles in terms of goals, programs created and abandoned, and cultural identity celebrated and strengthened. Indeed, the War on Poverty in Los Angeles lived longer and evolved in ways that would have surprised its planners, supporters, and detractors.

The Chicano movement, the black freedom struggle, the feminist movement, and the War on Poverty were intricately and fundamentally connected. Following the lead of Jacquelyn Dowd Hall, I argue for a "long civil rights movement," expanding the geographical, chronological, and organizational boundaries of struggles for racial and economic equality, for many of those who battled in the community-organization trenches of the War on Poverty had previously fought for black or Mexican American civil rights, labor-union representation, or women's rights. The community activists in the War on Poverty clearly viewed it as an extension of previous and future attempts to democratize America.[19]

This story is as much about race as it is about the War on Poverty; indeed, it can be read as a narrative about race in Los Angeles as seen through the prism of the War on Poverty. The story is essentially about how the racial status quo attempted to exclude large-scale participation by African Americans and Mexican Americans in the War on Poverty in Los Angeles, and how African Americans and Mexican Americans then challenged that racial order and redefined the meaning of race in Los Angeles by establishing their own antipoverty agencies in black and Mexican American communities.

In the process of doing so, tensions between Mexican Americans and African Americans at times reached dangerous levels. Seeing themselves as economic competitors for a dwindling supply of economic resources, blacks and Chicanos at times battled both within and without the structure of the War on Poverty. They shared a checkered history, with occasional attempts at interracial cooperation often giving way to distrust and competition. With the influence of culturally nationalist ideologies and a War on Poverty that emphasized *community control* of antipoverty programs, black/Chicano relationships during the period of the War on Poverty in Los Angeles were more about friction or distance than cooperation. Even so, occasional episodes of cooperation and affiliation occurred, providing examples of a complex and intricate relationship.[20]

As much as anything, these complicated relationships reflected the shifting boundaries of race in Los Angeles. As Mexican Americans became Chicanos and Negroes became blacks, Afro Americans, or African Americans, their racial, cultural, and economic identities merged, evolved, and challenged traditional definitions. The War on Poverty encouraged and helped give shape to these new boundaries, just as the new racial and cultural identities and ideologies changed the direction and meaning of the War on Poverty in the city.

While I use Jacquelyn Dowd Hall's argument for a "long civil rights movement," I also argue for the concept of a "long war on poverty." Many scholars have argued that not only did the War on Poverty fail, but that it ended in the 1970s with the demise of the OEO. I argue in this book that not only did the War on Poverty continue well beyond the 1970s, but that it is still being fought today in Los Angeles and in communities around the nation.[21]

While this book is about Los Angeles, many of its themes and issues echoed across the United States during the 1960s and 1970s. Politicians in other municipalities battled with community activists over control of War on Poverty funds; tensions grew between racial and ethnic communities in other American cities over the limited resources of the War on Poverty, and thousands of ethnically distinct neighborhood organizations, many of them created by women, sprung up across the United States as ordinary Americans tried to utilize the framework of the War on Poverty to democratize America and benefit their communities. Themes of racial separatism and interracial conflict, battles for community identity and economic resources, contests for the expansion of democracy, and attempts by ordinary people to define themselves, their communities, and their freedom, permeate the narratives of both Los Angeles and the nation as a whole during those tumultuous decades.

Chapter 1
African Americans, Civil Rights, and the Origins of the War on Poverty in Los Angeles

Los Angeles is not a paradise, much as the sight of its lilies and roses might lead one at first to believe. The color line is there sharply drawn.

W. E. B. Du Bois on visiting Los Angeles for the NAACP in 1913

Los Angeles City Government in the 1960s

A SMALL INTERRACIAL GROUP of 44 Mexican colonists formed the Spanish pueblo of Los Angeles in 1781. The pueblo grew slowly, and by the time of incorporation as a municipality of the United States in 1850, had well under 10,000 residents. Both Los Angeles and the state of California experienced a population boom in the late nineteenth century, with the city growing to over 100,000 inhabitants by 1900. By the mid-1960s, after another population explosion following the Second World War, Los Angeles had a population of almost 2.5 million and was geographically the largest city in the United States.[1]

In 1965 political scientist Edward Banfield wrote *Big City Politics*, a study of the structure and inner workings of politics in several of the largest cities in the United States, including Los Angeles. In his book Banfield demonstrated that Los Angeles city government consisted of a powerful city council, which controlled budgetary and planning issues; a decentralized administration containing nineteen independent departments headed by part-time boards; and a mayor with limited powers and no party affiliation, thus having no patronage system to manipulate. As a result of the decentralized system, issues that affected particular districts were usually solved. Issues that involved the entire city, however, were often ineffectively handled.[2] In fact, governmental authority was so dispersed that a "downtown elite," consisting of business owners and bankers such as Asa Call, Neil Petrie, and John Mc-

10

Cone held significant influence in many postwar decisions.[3] Los Angeles's weak mayoral government gave the city council power over many appointments, which made bureaucracies in the City of Angels more independent from mayoral control. On the other hand, power was so dispersed and mayoral opponents had such difficulty in building policy coalitions that the right person in the mayor's chair could still be the most powerful person in Los Angeles.[4]

Samuel William Yorty was determined to be the mayor to rise above those limitations on his power. Elected to the California State Assembly in 1936 as a liberal New Deal Democrat, Yorty joined the race for mayor of Los Angeles in 1938 but did not receive the nomination because he was considered too liberal. He shifted with the political winds in the early 1940s and became virulently anticommunist, a trait that would stay with him for the rest of his political career. Yorty suffered a number of political failures in the forties and fifties, which included losing elections for mayor, governor, lieutenant governor, and state senator. Always seen as something of a maverick, Yorty strengthened that image in 1960 with his publication of a pamphlet titled "I Can Not Take Kennedy," which attacked JFK's youth, wealth, and religion. He thought of Kennedy as "kind of a pretty boy" and instead supported Lyndon Johnson in 1960 for his "mature judgment, common sense, and qualities of leadership." Yorty went on to support Republican Richard Nixon in the general election, something that did not endear him to Johnson, despite the mayor's support of Johnson at the convention.[5]

Yorty campaigned successfully for mayor of Los Angeles in 1961 as an outsider and an opponent of the "power structure" (i.e., the downtown elite and the *Los Angeles Times*). He also appealed to suburban discontent by railing against poor refuse collection and overtaxation. In addition Yorty attempted to gain black votes by promising an end to police brutality. His refusal to keep that promise once he was in office and his association with racists alienated many African Americans. Instead of ending police brutality, Yorty defended the openly bigoted police chief, William Parker. In his 1969 campaign versus black city councilman Tom Bradley, Yorty used racist mailings and advertisements to court the white backlash vote. As mayor, Yorty continually butted heads with the city council in an effort to lessen their influence and increase the power of the mayor. He often held televised press conferences specifically to lash out at the council. The council, in turn, referred to Yorty as "paranoid," an "egomaniac," and a "would-be dictator."[6]

Yorty was clearly an annoyance to Johnson throughout his presidency, and Yorty's self-important personality dominates his correspondence with LBJ. Apparently, since he had supported Johnson, he believed the president owed him. He constantly gave LBJ unsolicited advice, as in 1967, when he advised LBJ to speed up the reading of his speeches because it was "much too draggy."[7] LBJ merely put up with him, but Yorty seemed to think he had a personal friendship with the president. In a June 1964 letter, Yorty sounded like a peevish child when he wrote to LBJ complaining that Johnson was making a campaign appearance in Los Angeles and had not informed Yorty about his specific plans. He told the president, "I am fed up with the stepchild treatment. If I am not at the Los Angeles dinner it will not hurt me because I will just tell the truth—that I was not invited. It might reflect unfavorably upon you, and that is the only reason I am writing."[8] Yorty's self-centeredness and self-importance also played a role in his spats with the city council and his political foes, including the local supporters of the War on Poverty.

African Americans in Los Angeles in the Early Sixties: Some Tenuous Gains

African Americans were among the first settlers in Los Angeles. Twenty-six of the forty-four original settlers in 1781 were black or black and Mexican; however, the black population in Los Angeles remained relatively small until early in the twentieth century. With the influx of whites and blacks in the early twentieth century, blacks in Los Angeles faced increased discrimination and segregation in all aspects of life, including jobs and housing. The suburb of Glendale, for instance, boasted in the 1920s that "no Negro ever sleeps overnight in our city." Racially restrictive covenants circumscribed blacks to the Central Avenue District and Watts, a residential area seven miles south of downtown Los Angeles. Surrounded by the all-white communities of South Gate, Lynwood, and Bell, residents of Watts faced economic, social, and spatial isolation.[9]

Black activists fought this repression from the outset. Charlotta Spears Bass helped her husband found the *California Eagle,* the first black-owned newspaper in California, in 1910 and crusaded against racial discrimination. Black residents in Los Angeles established a National Association for the Advancement of Colored People (NAACP) chapter in 1913, and local graduates of the Tuskegee Institute founded the Los Angeles Urban League in 1921 to promote integration. Leon Washington established another black newspaper, the *Los Angeles Sentinel,* in the early 1930s. Its masthead read, "Don't spend where you can't work."[10]

Civil rights organizations in Los Angeles experienced a significant upsurge in the 1940s with the mass migration of African Americans to the West, particularly to Los Angeles, for war-industry jobs. Between 1940 and 1946, the African American population of Los Angeles expanded by 70,000. Likewise, membership in civil rights organizations in Los Angeles burgeoned dramatically during the war and immediate postwar years.[11]

By the early 1960s the decentralized, splintered system of government and politics in Los Angeles plus a mayor focused on aggrandizing his own power made it difficult for minority groups to gain much influence. The division of authority between city and county, the weak mayor-council tradition, the nonpartisan elections, and the lack of an urban political machine, with its tradition of service and welfare, all added up to a powerful roadblock for civil rights groups to overcome. The Los Angeles governmental system was designed to reduce the influence of elected officials over the resources of government that minority groups needed to make some headway. A splintered, decentralized system of government and a racist police chief and mayor combined to prevent minority groups from "gaining sufficient political resources to achieve significant levels of participation."[12]

Furthermore, many civil rights organizations in Los Angeles lacked substantial support. In 1960, over 350,000 blacks lived in Los Angeles, yet the Los Angeles chapter of the NAACP boasted a total of only 8,000 members, a significant decline from its peak of 14,000 in 1945, when it had been the fifth-largest chapter in the United States. The Red Scare of the 1950s greatly contributed to that downturn, completely destroying the left-liberal Civil Rights Congress in Los Angeles and dramatically weakening the local NAACP. Within the NAACP, an anticommunist slate won the chapter elections in 1955, stripping the branch of some its white members and making it less likely to take controversial stands. Indeed, chapter president Thomas Neusom reported that his first official act in 1955 was to call a special meeting of the board of directors to present "a resolution placing this administration on record as opposing the membership in this branch of all persons who were known to be or that we could establish were members of the Communist Party." The board of directors unanimously approved Neusom's resolution. As a result of the purges that followed, the chapter became a relatively conservative middle-class organization consisting primarily of preachers, doctors, and lawyers and did not appeal to most working-class blacks. In addition, the NAACP's general tendency for court action over mass action kept it from gaining a broad working-class base. Thus, class differences within Los Angeles's black community often hindered it from presenting a unified front on issues of concern to many African Americans, such as an antipoverty agency.[13]

Despite some weak organizational support, civil rights organizations in Los Angeles did make some advances in the early 1960s. The Reverend H. H. Brookins was one reason why. In late 1960 Brookins arrived from Wichita, Kansas, to be the new pastor of the First African Methodist Episcopal [AME] Church in Los Angeles. He and other civil rights activists formed the biracial (black and white) United Civil Rights Committee (UCRC) following an appearance in Los Angeles in 1963 by the Reverend Martin Luther King, Jr. In the early 1960s Brookins and other members of the UCRC prodded city leaders on issues including housing, education, and law enforcement. Brookins's leadership, along with that of Tom Bradley, helped unite blacks, at least temporarily, in the early 1960s. African Americans gained representation on the city council as well as some power in mayoral elections.[14]

The first significant effort at black political mobilization occurred in 1960–61, when African Americans attempted to influence the reapportionment process based on the 1960 census. Black activists such as Brookins and black-owned newspapers, including the *Los Angeles Sen-*

tinel, lobbied for two state senate and four assembly seats to be created in heavily black districts. Instead, African American districts received only one senate and two assembly seats. In the city reapportionment, the city council divided black neighborhoods and created only one district with a black majority.[15]

Disappointed with the results of reapportionment, the black community made a second attempt to gain political power in 1961. The tenth district council seat came up for appointment, and Tom Bradley, a former Los Angeles Police Department (LAPD) officer, campaigned for the council nomination. The council, however, refused to nominate an African American, despite Bradley's popularity among both blacks and whites in his district. This defeat only unified black Angelenos more, and in 1963 they came together (with additional support from white liberals) to elect Bradley to represent the tenth district, Billy Mills the eighth district, and Gilbert Lindsay the ninth district. Suddenly, African Americans in Los Angeles had three representatives on the city council.[16]

Those electoral victories, though, were tempered somewhat by an apparent widening of class differences among African Americans. Class distinctions historically had never been as significant for blacks as for whites, since African Americans had generally not been allowed to participate fully in the American economy. Class differences among African Americans tended to center on lifestyle and values, or perhaps established residents versus newcomers, more than income. The World War II and postwar economic boom created more wealth for many African Americans, relatively speaking, as well as certain class distinctions based more on income, home ownership, and other economic variables than in the period prior to World War II. Some African Americans took advantage of their newfound ability to purchase homes in the suburbs, which created some class divisions in the political representation of blacks in Los Angeles. For instance, the tenth district, represented by Bradley, consisted primarily of an upwardly mobile black middle class in the Baldwin Hills area, about ten miles west of South Central Los Angeles. The eighth council district, represented by Mills, consisted primarily of lower-income, unemployed, and underemployed blacks in South Central Los Angeles. At times this physical separation of the black middle class in Baldwin Hills from the central city created additional social and political factionalism.[17]

The men who represented those districts were similar to the people they represented and could not have been more different from each other. Bradley, a former policeman, was highly educated, liberal, and smooth; he was part of the reform wing of the Democratic Party and emphasized compromise over confrontation. Bradley's biographers note that when he was elected to the council, he "was determined to lead Los Angeles away from . . . confrontational tactics. . . . He would have to . . . be prepared to utilize his skills at mediation." Bradley himself stated, "I am councilman of the entire district, not one group of people." In fact Bradley was part of a biracial coalition of black and white liberal elites that gained power and would help elect Bradley mayor in 1969. Mills, on the other hand, was direct, confrontational, and rough around the edges; he opposed the reform wing of the Democratic Party and represented the black working class.[18]

Somewhat buoyed by their electoral success, civil rights organizations united in a campaign to end segregation in Los Angeles. In 1963 the Congress of Racial Equality (CORE), the NAACP, and Brookins and the UCRC held several civil rights marches through downtown in an attempt to end segregated schools in Los Angeles and organized the opposition to Proposition 14, which would repeal the Rumford Fair Housing Act. Because of racially restrictive covenants, many African Americans in Los Angeles were forced to live in the South Central section of Los Angeles, especially Watts.[19] The tiny lot sizes in that area limited the size and quality of homes built there. A handful of upwardly mobile blacks were able to move to nearby suburbs, such as Baldwin Hills, but most remained trapped in inadequate housing in Watts. The Rumford Fair Housing Act had been intended to end housing discrimination in California, and when it passed the California legislature, many blacks hailed the legislation as a great victory for their community. The jubilation did not last long. Real-estate interests formed an anti-Rumford coalition that forced the measure before the state voters as Proposition 14. Civil rights groups throughout California opposed the measure, but their efforts to defeat it failed miserably, as Prop 14 passed by a 2-1 margin statewide and in Los Angeles County. The success of Prop 14 discouraged many blacks from participation in the political process. The presence of three black members on the city council in Los Angeles had not thwarted housing discrimination.[20]

The elections of Bradley, Lindsay, and Mills may have been due to more to compound racism than to the political strength of the African American community. Local elites were more frightened by the size and strength of the Latino population than that of African American residents and may have been willing to support black candidates as a result. Those candidates, particularly Bradley and Lindsay, were part of the establishment and often hesitated to directly confront it, their position within the establishment at times neutralizing their commitment to seeking solutions for poor blacks.[21]

Thus, by 1964 civil rights organizations had won three city council seats but had lost in their efforts to challenge segregated housing and schools in Los Angeles. Undeterred by these losses, or perhaps because of them, civil rights organizations in Los Angeles in 1964–65 began to turn their attention to the newly created War on Poverty. Once the Economic Opportunity Act was created and the legislation was signed by President Johnson, minority groups in Los Angeles actively sought to use the legislation, implementing it in ways that would benefit and empower the minority poor.

Los Angeles in the 1960s remained a community with a decentralized city government that had problems effectively dealing with citywide issues. Its city government was embroiled in bitter mayor-versus-council battles. It was a city with some fledgling, growing civil rights organizations, but those groups were only tenuously united. Political and class divisions within the African American community would play a significant role not only in the growing black freedom struggle, but also in the unfolding drama of the War on Poverty in Los Angeles.

The Youth Opportunities Board:
"You are going to make history with this one"

The local War on Poverty in Los Angeles had the same roots as the national one. Both descended directly from the federal government's interest in juvenile delinquency and the creation of the Committee on

Juvenile Delinquency in 1961. The committee based its fight against juvenile delinquency on the "opportunity theory" of Columbia University sociologists Richard Cloward and Lloyd Ohlin. According to Ohlin and Cloward's theory, juvenile delinquency resulted from societal structures such as unresponsive school systems, uncaring welfare administrations, and inattentive city governments that blocked the opportunities and aspirations of inner-city adolescents. Ohlin and Cloward argued that the opportunity structure differed in each community; therefore, each community required different services. An executive order charged the committee with establishing a federal grant program to help state and local agencies combat juvenile delinquency.[22]

In the spring of 1961, shortly after the creation of the Juvenile Delinquency Committee, a national conference was held in Washington, D.C., to discuss the issue. Karl Holton, the chief probation officer of Los Angeles County, attended the conference. Upon his return to Los Angeles, he tried to mobilize public and private groups (city and county schools, Catholic Social Services, the YMCA, etc.) in the area to provide service programs directed toward juveniles. Many were ready to listen, as concerns about rising dropout, unemployment, and delinquency rates were widespread at the time. The number of juvenile delinquency cases nationwide had increased 137 percent from 1948 to 1957. In addition, Tennessee senator Estes Kefauver had created a subcommittee in 1955 to study juvenile delinquency. The subcommittee hearings focused on headline-grabbing topics such as violence and sex in the media and sensationalized the issue of juvenile delinquency, which raised concern in communities throughout the nation. In January 1962 county supervisor Ernest Debs called a Conference on Youth for the Los Angeles area. At the conference Robert Goe, executive assistant to Los Angeles mayor Sam Yorty, concerned with both the issue of juvenile delinquency and enhancing his boss's prestige, proposed creating a Joint Powers Agreement between the city and the county to create an agency to combat juvenile delinquency.[23]

While negotiations continued regarding a Joint Powers Agreement, city and county staff began working on a proposal to present to the Juvenile Delinquency Committee. In March Goe met with David

Hackett and Richard Boone, two Juvenile Delinquency Committee staff members, to discuss the proposal in the works for Los Angeles. Goe wrote to Yorty: "Both men [Hackett and Boone] believe that this is the most significant step to be taken anywhere in the United States to attack the problems of youth unemployment and delinquency, and assured me that the Joint Powers Board will receive their complete cooperation. . . .You are going to make history with this one."[24]

The city and county signed a Joint Powers Agreement on April 3, 1962, to create the Youth Opportunities Board of Greater Los Angeles (YOB). Representatives from the City of Los Angeles, County of Los Angeles, the California Department of Employment, the Los Angeles Unified School District, and the Los Angeles Junior College District signed the agreement. The board, consisting of one member from each organization, included a Community Agency Advisory Committee comprised of representatives of agencies such as the Boys Club, the Welfare Planning Council (a group of predominantly African American social workers), the Urban League, the Catholic Welfare Bureau, and the Council of Mexican-American Affairs. YOB—which also included a Citizens Advisory Committee, with representatives from industry, labor, churches, and civic groups—was not created as an agency to implement programs, but as a means to coordinate the facilities and resources of existing organizations.[25]

One of the stated goals of YOB was to create self-help and mutual-help organizations such as child-care cooperatives. It established Information and Complaint Outposts, including one in Watts operated by the Los Angeles Urban League, through which workers operated as troubleshooters or neighborhood advocates to provide a link between services and people. Many residents believed these outposts met at least some of their needs. Participants and residents surveyed claimed that services were better coordinated and delivered under the YOB than they had been previously under traditional city and county agencies.[26] Yet provision of services and the active inclusion of area residents in the development of the program were two very different things. In reality YOB remained in the exclusive control of the state and local government agencies that Ohlin and Cloward had criticized and which the Juvenile Delinquency Committee was supposed to prod to change or completely remove from the process. That control would be challenged with the creation and implementation of the War on Poverty.

Warring over Poverty

The theory behind the War on Poverty was the same "opportunity theory" that underlay the purpose of the Juvenile Delinquency Committee. Policymakers argued that societal structures blocked opportunities for the poor and assumed that many of the grant recipients would be the same agencies that had received money from the Juvenile Delinquency Committee. Local government leaders in Los Angeles, who by 1964 were more invested in YOB, assumed the same thing. They immediately began making plans to include OEO programs in the Youth Opportunities Board.

In a memo to the mayor and city council, city administrative officer C. Erwin Piper listed the Job Corps, work-study programs, and community-action programs as projects that would benefit Los Angeles. Interestingly, he defined a community-action program as "one that mobilizes and utilizes public or private resources to provide service [and] assistance."[27] His definition, not surprising given the vague wording, completely ignored the "maximum feasible participation" of the poor. It was clear from the start that representation of the poor on the city's community-action agency would not be important to city leaders.

While city administrators had their own ideas of how to implement the War on Poverty, black leaders were also excited by the new legislation and intended to ensure what they saw as the proper implementation of the poverty program. The *Los Angeles Sentinel* editorialized: "It is gratifying to know a large portion of [the War on Poverty] is designed to boost the living standards and earning potential of the millions of minority citizens who are included in the 'forgotten fifth' of our nation's population. . . . We must make sure that some of its benefits come to communities like ours where its objectives are vitally needed."[28]

Councilman Bradley presented a motion adopted by the city council to explore the means for implementation and participation in the community-action phase of the War on Poverty. In presenting the motion, he argued that "government at the local level must play a vital role in developing the Anti-Poverty Program." In doing so, Bradley continued, local government "must work cooperatively" with community agencies.[29] The community agencies Bradley mentioned undoubtedly included the Welfare Planning Council, which had supported Bradley in his campaign. While Bradley seemed to ignore the participation of the poor in his statement (he mentioned the role of local government and community agencies, but not the individual poor), he and other black leaders saw the War on Poverty as something that could be used for the benefit of African Americans.

African American leaders generally supported the War on Poverty but also challenged Piper's assumption of traditional agency control and his definition of community action, and they wanted to ensure the participation of African Americans in the initiative. The black freedom movement and the War on Poverty both sought to open the doors of opportunity for African Americans. African Americans in Los Angeles clearly saw the War on Poverty framework as a means by which to achieve the economic, social, and political goals of the black freedom movement, but at times they disagreed over the structure and control of the War on Poverty.

Shortly after the creation of OEO, a group of black professionals began to meet at the home of Opal Jones, a social worker and member of the Welfare Planning Council and the Los Angeles Area Federation of Settlements and Neighborhood Centers (LAAFSNC), to discuss the reform of Los Angeles's welfare system. Jones was the executive director of the Avalon Community Center, a United Way agency and a member of the Federation of Settlements, formed in 1963. City councilman Tom Bradley served as president of the center. This group of black professionals (many of whom belonged to the Federation of Settlements and/or the Welfare Planning Council) decided to prevent the local government agencies from controlling the implementation of the War on Poverty in Los Angeles. They expressed concern that Mayor Yorty would attempt to control the program and prevent significant African American participation. Also, OEO was considering applications for community-action agency status and War on Poverty funds from both private and public agencies. These African American, middle-class professionals, both men and women, created the Economic Opportunity Federation (EOF), a private agency, to compete with EYOA to be the Community Action Agency for Los Angeles. The EOF proposal to OEO, "The War on Poverty Must Be Joined in the Neighborhood: A Community Action Proposal of the Los Angeles Area Federation of Settlements and Neighborhood Centers," listed as its objectives neighborhood organization, family-centered resources, volunteer training, and jobs programs. EOF was supported by the Welfare Planning Council and the LAAFSNC as well as several congressmen from the Los Angeles area, including Augustus Hawkins, Edward Roybal, James Roosevelt, and George E. Brown, Jr. (all liberal reform Democrats and "bitter political foes of Yorty").[30]

Yorty took the creation of EOF as a personal and political affront. As he saw it, a group of citizens had created an organization to challenge his political power. His opposition to the new agency was in part a principled stand against the participatory aspect of the War on Poverty. Yorty believed that as an elected public official, he should be able to control the organization; thus, his representative model of democracy conflicted with the participatory vision of the War on Poverty. Yorty's opposition, however, was as much selfish as principled—he did not want to risk losing any political power. In a letter to President Johnson, Yorty complained about the conflict arising in Los Angeles over the administration of the War on Poverty and the fact that EOF was attempting to remove the city from local control of it. Walter Jenkins, special assistant to Johnson, responded that he was "sorry to hear that you have problems, and I will look into them and see what can be done."[31]

The conflict between EOF and Yorty began to cost Los Angeles money, and in the meantime the poor lost opportunities for employment, job training, and services. In November OEO granted $2.7 million to YOB for job-training programs, but it withheld disbursement of the funds because YOB did not meet OEO criteria for representation of the poor. Unfortunately, the groups involved still were unable to reach an agreement on their own.[32]

In January 1965, after two more months of delays caused in large part by Yorty's reluctance to compromise, the federal government responded by suggesting its own compromise. OEO recommended that

EOF and YOB merge and include more low-income representatives on the board, expanding the board of the merged group to twenty-two members (ten public-agency, six private-agency, and six community representatives).[33] OEO hoped that the compromise and the increase in the number of community representatives would solve the conflict.

It seemed to work, at least at first. In February YOB and EOF set aside their differences and approved the merger. Indeed, a YOB report, "The War on Poverty in Los Angeles," issued in April 1965 hailed the merger with EOF as a way to provide "broader community representation." The public and private agencies would join forces to form the Economic and Youth Opportunities Agency of Greater Los Angeles (EYOA). Many key political figures also supported the merger. Congressman Hawkins saw it as a way to get federal money to projects in Los Angeles, noting that "unless something is done soon, Los Angeles will lose millions of dollars of federal funds and widespread dissension will result."[34] The EOF/YOB conflict appeared to be over.

Mayor Yorty, however, continued his attempts to gain power. Despite the fact that both EOF and YOB approved OEO's solution, he remained unwilling to accept the proposed merger. Angered over the fact that the number of private citizens (twelve) would outnumber the public servants (ten) on the proposed board, Yorty blasted the OEO-proposed merger in a message to the city council. He argued that "12 private citizens . . . would be placed in a position where they could establish public policy and control the expenditure of public funds without having to account to the electorate."[35] Yorty's real concern, however, remained that he could not control community representatives as well as he could control city representatives. Indeed, one scholar has concluded that the mayor "sought to undermine the poverty war in Los Angeles by packing his cronies on the YOB."[36]

Instead of following the OEO compromise, Yorty offered his own proposal. It allowed for a merger of the two groups, but the board was to consist of only nine members, all city and county representatives.[37] In the name of protecting taxpayers and preventing public criticism, Yorty was determined to retain control of YOB; indeed, he "figuratively stood in the door of City Hall blocking the distribution of federal anti-poverty funds."[38]

In response, some community and civic leaders formed a Community Anti-Poverty Committee (CAPC) to study the proposed merger and overcome the impasse. The committee consisted of Congressman Gus Hawkins; Reverend Brookins; Norman Houston, the head of the Los Angeles chapter of the NAACP; Rev. Thomas Kilgore, the head of CORE's Los Angeles chapter; and other leaders and representatives from the city's diverse black community, including a number of women. Many of the members of the CAPC, such as Archie Hardwick of the Westminster Neighborhood Association and Arthur Takei of the Japanese-American Community Services Agency, were also members of EOF, the Federation of Settlements, or the Welfare Planning Council. Several Mexican Americans also joined the CAPC, including Tony Rios, the head of the Los Angeles chapter of the Community Service Organization, although the membership was predominantly black. The fact that this was a largely black organization was also reflected in the five areas the CAPC argued needed "immediate attention" from the War on Poverty: Avalon, Compton, Florence, downtown Los Angeles, and Watts —all neighborhoods with significantly high black populations. The CAPC quickly organized and created subcommittees on topics they saw as related to poverty—housing, small business development, public facilities improvement, education and training, and so forth—and held public meetings to ensure broad community input and support.[39]

Not surprisingly, the committee opposed Yorty's proposal, which demanded that the joint powers (i.e., the city and county) control the board. The CAPC argued that the agency needed more representation of the poor and a smaller number of government representatives on the board. They made their own proposal for a thirty-two-member board, including eighteen nongovernment representatives. The CAPC placed the blame for the local War on Poverty "mess directly on the shoulders of the joint powers and particularly Mayor Samuel Yorty and the Los Angeles City Council," arguing that Yorty and the city council had "obstructed" all attempts to make the antipoverty board representative of the poor. According to the CAPC, the city council had been "pressured and coerced" to approve Yorty's proposal, through which, they argued, Yorty "systematically and maliciously" planned to control all appointments and projects. Brookins accused Yorty of "playing politics with poverty."[40]

The CAPC pursued its goal of a representative antipoverty agency vigorously. Hawkins wrote OEO to clarify "whether public and private agencies together with representative community groups from poverty areas can proceed to organize an acceptable agency in event a city decides not to participate." In an article in the *Los Angeles Sentinel,* one of the CAPC's members, Dr. J. Alfred Cannon, associate director of the Social and Community Psychiatry Department at UCLA, eloquently appealed for black community involvement and issued an eerily prophetic warning:

If the community does not involve itself in this program, one of the greatest pieces of social legislation is doomed to failure. Not only will this tremendous piece of legislation die, but it in its wake, many other worthy programs will be strangled in the wave of public anger and disenchantment over the Anti-Poverty Program failure. The taste of failure is long-lasting and bitter. Two groups will be singled out with blame for its failure— minority staff members . . . and "deprived" and minority persons themselves [who] will be labeled as "not ready," "too resistant," "ungrateful," "wish to be poor." A piece of imaginative legislation could become one of the most divisive instrumentalities this country has ever known and cause horrendous community disruption. [41]

Cannon and the CAPC clearly saw the War on Poverty as a continuation, or "second wave," of the civil rights movement. They had given notice that they realized the potential of the War on Poverty to expand democracy and racial and economic equality, and they were going to attempt to ensure that it was implemented with the "maximum feasible participation" of the poor, as the legislation prescribed. They also understood that failure to do so could have dire consequences. They would not back down from Yorty.[42]

In response to the protests of the CAPC and others, Yorty announced his plans to appoint Councilman Billy Mills as the city representative to the EYOA board. This appointment of a black councilman was supposed to calm the CAPC members, but they knew that Mills was connected politically to Yorty and would serve as Yorty's rubber stamp on the board. Furthermore, Yorty did not back down from his proposal.[43]

Community leaders stood their ground. They continued to reject Yorty's proposal and his plan for an advisory board, which the leaders believed would reject community proposals before they got to the EYOA board. In addition, Congressmen Hawkins, Roosevelt, Roybal, and Brown asked OEO to bypass EYOA and fund local projects directly, and they wanted the joint powers to accept the poor as equal partners in the antipoverty agency. According to Hawkins, the situation had "reached a crisis stage in Los Angeles County, a crisis caused by the failure of public agencies."[44]

The issue came to a head in a tense city-council chamber on July 8, 1965. The council met to vote on a new Joint Powers Agreement (JPA) with the county in order to create the EYOA officially. The updated proposal included a board of nineteen members—ten from public agencies, six community representatives, and three from private organizations. The community representatives were to be appointed by the mayor and the Los Angeles County Board of Supervisors. The proposal had Yorty's backing, because it maintained public-agency dominance in total numbers of representatives. It also kept agency control over the selection of community representatives.[45]

Representatives of seven different community agencies, including the CAPC, expressed their opposition to the proposed compromise. At a city council meeting on July 8, 1965, they argued that it would exclude representation of the poor. They also supported the election, rather than the appointment, of community representatives. They believed that the EOF proposal would allow for more community control and better delivery of service programs than the JPA proposal, but the primary issue remained representation of the poor.[46]

Others from the community, however, supported the merger. Rev. William Carpenter and Edward Weise argued that it was better to compromise and receive some kind of CAA, than to delay too long and risk not receiving an OEO grant at all. OEO was still holding back the funds it had granted EYOA in 1964, because EYOA had not met the requirements for representation of the poor. They had offered no guarantee as to how long they would wait before rescinding their offer. Faced with strong opposing forces, the city council balked. They tabled the proposal and sent the issue back to committee.[47]

Meanwhile, Yorty attempted to make a backroom deal. Yorty was being opposed by James Roosevelt in the 1965 mayoral election and had been pestering President Johnson for his support for almost a year. Under pressure from OEO to sign the agreement, Yorty tried to get LBJ to agree to a deal whereby Johnson would appoint Roosevelt to the UN, thus getting him out of Yorty's way, and Yorty would sign the agreement. Johnson was not biting. He considered the issue a local one.[48]

The Board of Supervisors also considered the merger. On July 13, by a 3-2 vote, they approved the JPA with an amendment adding three additional community representatives to the board, as well as nonvoting representatives from the United Way, the League of California Cities, and the Los Angeles Area Chamber of Commerce. City Councilmen Mills and Lindsay supported the board's action; the CAPC opposed it.[49]

Outside the County Hall of Administration, a predominantly African American gathering of a few thousand marched and carried signs denouncing the city and county government and protesting the official agency proposals as being unrepresentative of the poor and minorities. Brookins and Rev. Martin Luther King, Jr., led the demonstrations. King had come to Los Angeles specifically to show support for Brookins's thirty-two-member poverty-board plan. In a press conference, King spoke in measured tones about the need for true "maximum feasible participation" and implicitly attacked Yorty: "I hope . . . that the poverty bill will not be used by any officials of government for their own patronage but will be used for the people for which it is intended. . . . If this poverty bill is to have meaning in the community, the people who have been victimized will have to have a part in the shaping of the program and their own destinies."[50]

Rev. Brookins sounded more agitated in his remarks, which he directed at the black community of Los Angeles. Disappointed that more people had not shown up to demonstrate, Brookins noted that he was "appalled at the apathy" of the African American community. He lashed out at the black poor for "sitting by while local politicians swindle them out of millions in poverty programs aimed at bettering their lives."[51]

King and Brookins demonstrated that at least some civil rights leaders saw the War on Poverty as a way to help bring about economic and racial justice and an expansion of American democracy. They clearly saw the War on Poverty framework as one that could help achieve some of the democratic goals of the civil rights movement. The focus remained on inclusion and representation, but issues such as cultural identity and group empowerment were emerging as important factors.

Not all members of the black community, however, agreed with King and Brookins; indeed, members of Brookins's ministerial fraternity in Los Angeles disagreed vehemently with him on the structure and control of Los Angeles's War on Poverty. A few days after the protest in front of the County Hall of Administration, a group of black ministers met to discuss the War on Poverty stalemate. They never came close to an agreement. In a meeting rife with personal attacks, the ministers voted 43-26 to accept the Yorty proposal and, in effect, show their support for Councilman Mills. The vote reflected some of the growing class tensions among African Americans as well as differing perspectives on the direction of the black freedom movement. The Reverend E. V. Hill, the conservative pastor of Mt. Zion Baptist Church, led the supporters of this proposal. Hill had openly backed Yorty in the 1963 election and remained close to him throughout his tenure as mayor (Hill later received funding from EYOA for organizing an antipoverty project). Rev. Brookins led the opposition to the Yorty proposal, and when the proposal won, a statement approved by a majority of the ministers attacked Brookins. In an attempt to turn the tables on Brookins, the ministers accused him of "attempting to block all funds until the five local levels of government agree to go along with a program meeting his personal approval, even if it means the poor have to suffer in the meantime."[52] In this scenario it was not Yorty, but Brookins, who stood in the doorway, blocking the OEO funds.

Thus, as the summer of 1965 wore on, the black community remained divided over the issue of community representation and political power. The ministerial vote on the War on Poverty reflected some of the growing class tensions among African Americans as well as differing perspectives on the direction of the movement for civil rights. But the clash over the control of the War on Poverty in Los Angeles was about to take a dramatic turn.

The political battling over the war on poverty raged into August. On August 10 Congressman Hawkins held a one-day hearing of a subcommittee of the House Committee on Education and Labor to investigate the War on Poverty stalemate in Los Angeles. Over one thousand Angelenos gathered at the Will Rogers Park auditorium to witness the proceedings. During and after the hearing, the ministerial and political contest continued. Hill, the chairman of Mayor Yorty's Committee on Economic Opportunity, called Hawkins's hearing "biased and one-sided" and announced that the mayor would continue with his plans for EYOA. Brookins, representing the CAPC, argued that the hearing served as a necessary venue for the poor to "express their will" and that any Yorty plan remained unacceptable. On August 11 the *Times* reported that the poor were still "waiting outside . . . while Mayor Samuel W. Yorty and Representative Augustus F. Hawkins . . . accuse each other of attempting to seize political control of the program."[53] An editorial in the *Sentinel* the same day blasted Yorty for using "every whit of tomfoolery, invective and misleading insinuations . . . to cast aspersions on . . . anybody . . . who dared to challenge" him in the War on Poverty battle. The paper blamed that stalemate on Yorty and others in "the local power structure who fear that allowing the actual poor to help in planning and directing a program to lessen their misery would pose a threat to established political leadership."[54] Neither the *Times* nor the *Sentinel* stories made the front page. No one would overlook the headlines the following day.

In early August 1965, one year after the official declaration of the War on Poverty, the city of Los Angeles still waited for its War on Poverty to begin. A self-interested, stubborn mayor and an entrenched white establishment had locked horns with small but increasingly vocal minority and civil rights groups intent on having a voice in the implementation of the War on Poverty and creating more widespread community participation. Though these groups had not requested a War on Poverty, they had determined to use the legislation to expand opportunities for low-income minorities. These groups, however, were united tenuously. In fact, the black community, as evidenced by the actions of the black ministers, was as divided as it was united. Political and class divisions, as well as differences over compromise versus confrontation, would continue to hinder the strength of minority groups in Los Angeles and the implementation of the War on Poverty. And the apathy that so angered the Reverend Brookins was about to end.

Chapter 2
Struggles for Black Empowerment in Watts

Watts and Its Aftermath

AT APPROXIMATELY SEVEN P.M. on the warm evening of Wednesday, August 11, a white California highway patrolman stopped Marquette Frye and his brother Ronald, both African Americans, along with their two female companions, at 166th Street near Avalon in South Central Los Angeles, under suspicion of drunken driving. The Fryes and their friends had spent the better part of the afternoon celebrating the end of Marquette's service in the air force. A verbal confrontation that included the Fryes' mother, Rena, ensued with the patrolmen. A crowd gathered. When the patrolman and additional officers who had arrived on the scene became violent in their handling of the Fryes, some in the crowd threw rocks. More police officers were called in, and violence erupted between the officers and the growing crowd. What began on August 11 as a routine traffic stop set off five days of anger, violence, burning, and destruction. When the tumult finally ended, thirty-four people were dead (most were African American), over one thousand were injured, more than eleven thousand were arrested, and over $35 million in property was destroyed. Some of the most significant damage occurred on 103rd Avenue, the main commercial center of Watts, but much of the violence took place outside of Watts, in other sections of South Central Los Angeles. Over thirty-five thousand residents of South Central Los Angeles took part, and President Johnson called in more than sixteen thousand National Guardsmen to quell the revolt.[1]

Immediately, scholars and journalists conducted dozens of studies to determine why Watts had happened. Most called it a riot, some thought it a revolution, but most analysts agreed that police brutality was the primary reason for the revolt. That the Los Angeles Police

31

Department was perhaps the most virulently racist, brutally violent big-city police department in the United States was not a new revelation to most black Angelenos in 1965. The LAPD was renowned for arresting African Americans for no reason, concocting rationales for the arrest, and brutally beating "suspects." When running for mayor in 1961, Sam Yorty had promised African Americans an end to police brutality. After his election, however, he had a private meeting with Police Chief William Parker and never made any attempt to control police violence. Rumors circulated that Parker had some personal information on Yorty that he used to keep the mayor in his corner. Following the meeting and throughout his tenure as mayor, Yorty made little effort to control police violence or brutality. In June of 1962 a group of black ministers met with Yorty to discuss claims of police brutality. Calling Parker "anti-Negro," they asked Yorty "to take immediate steps" to investigate the police department and Parker "in order to avoid dire consequences in the community." Yorty ignored their claims. A team of investigators from the U.S. Commission on Civil Rights visited South Central later that year and, after listening to testimony from individuals and organizations, including the NAACP, CORE, the Southern California Council of Churches, and the California Democratic Council, charged the LAPD with police brutality. The committee's report noted the "surprisingly hostile" reaction to them by city officials (primarily Yorty and Parker). Yorty vigorously denounced the committee's charges and referred to the investigators as communists—his empty promises to end police brutality had been made simply to obtain votes from the black community.[2]

Yorty's denial of claims of police brutality did not improve blacks' opinion of the LAPD. In 1963 YOB surveyed attitudes toward the major service agencies in Los Angeles and found the greatest hostility toward the police department.[3] In May 1964, after conducting its own study, CORE called for Parker's resignation. CORE's report noted: "Los Angeles is faced with an emergency situation arising from the sharply increased tension between the police department and the minority communities. Minority dissatisfaction with police attitudes and methods is long-standing and for the past several years individual attorneys and civil rights organizations have warned of the growing cri-

Los Angeles mayor Sam Yorty and police chief William Parker answer questions from the press during the Watts uprising. Courtesy Los Angeles Public Library.

sis." In January 1965 CORE attempted a sit-in in the mayor's office to renew its demand that Parker resign, but Yorty and other city officials ignored CORE's warning and the problem festered until August 11.[4]

Mayor Yorty was partly to blame for the seriousness of the problem—he clearly ignored his city's racial problems. In September of 1964, he told reporters that black-white relations were better in Los Angeles than in any other major city. Hopelessly out of touch with the black residents of his city, Yorty made little effort to understand the racial divisions within Los Angeles or to discuss seriously blacks' concerns about Parker. When, years after the fact, he was asked to explain Watts, he blamed television coverage of the civil rights movement in the South. He never understood the underlying causes of the revolt.[5]

Yorty's contribution to the Watts revolt, however, was not just his indifference and implicit acceptance of police brutality and racism. Even more, it was his unwillingness to settle the local War on Poverty stalemate. Many early commentators noted that the inability of Los Angeles to agree on a Community Action Agency was a contributing factor to the Watts conflagration. Few, however, considered it a primary influence. Indeed, one of the early studies discounted the notion that disappointment in the poverty program was at all related to the revolt.[6] The EYOA fiasco, however, constituted a significant factor in the Watts revolt. The problems surrounding the poverty program in Los Angeles, particularly Yorty's refusal to compromise and allow more resident representation on the local antipoverty board, had been a key issue leading to the revolt. Yorty's support of Parker and his hindrance of the War on Poverty in Los Angeles were "powerful pre-conditions of the riot."[7]

Poverty was an issue as the majority of the residents in Watts were poor. Ninety percent of Watts residents were black, and two-thirds were on welfare; 34 percent of adult males were unemployed. Over 40 percent of Watts residents, a much higher percentage than in any other area of the city, lived in families with incomes below the poverty level. The purchasing power of the average family in South Central declined four hundred dollars a year between 1959 and 1965, and the average family in Watts earned only 52 percent of the national family income average. Nearly one-third of housing in South Central in 1965 was considered "dilapidated" or "deteriorating," compared to an average of 8 percent in Los Angeles County.[8]

Commentators of various political persuasions recognized the connection between the failure of the poverty program and the Watts revolt. The communist W.E.B. Du Bois Club of Los Angeles argued that poverty and the failure of the city of Los Angeles to comply with OEO requirements comprised one of the major reasons for the Watts revolt. In their list of recommendations on how to solve the problems in

Los Angeles, second behind the ouster of Chief Parker was the removal of obstacles to War on Poverty funding. The Los Angeles chapter of the NAACP urged several steps, but first was the establishment of an operating antipoverty program.[9]

The McCone Commission report, chaired by John McCone, a former CIA director and Los Angeles native, blamed publicity promising action from the poverty programs for the revolt. When those programs were delayed due to political bickering, people felt betrayed. The President's Task Force on the Los Angeles Riots reported that people in the poverty areas felt voiceless in community affairs. When the community action agency, which was supposed to provide a vehicle for them to be heard, never materialized, they revolted.[10]

Many politicians and public officials recognized the importance of the War on Poverty to the violence in Watts. Many of those officials "reported that unfulfilled promises of help from antipoverty funds . . . had proved a serious blunder leading to great frustration. Most blamed lack of anti-poverty funds on the political conflicts among public officials with some accusing Mayor Yorty of major blame."[11]

Gus Hawkins wrote Ramsey Clark that the delay in antipoverty funding comprised "part of the basic cause in the recent Los Angeles disorders."[12] In his testimony to the McCone Commission, Hawkins argued that "had politics not been played with anti-poverty funds, more youths would have been in meaningful activities this past summer, more indigenous leaders would have been in neighborhood programs, and more job-creating activities would have been in operation the early part of this year."[13] In a letter to Johnson advisor Jack Valenti, state senator Jesse Unruh asked Valenti to "use whatever influence you can to get the War on Poverty program moving in Los Angeles."[14] Republican senator George Murphy telegrammed OEO Director Sargent Shriver, "situation in Los Angeles makes it absolutely essential that poverty funds be released to that city. . . . Because of the critical situation, I strongly urge that you personally go to Los Angeles to this confusion and political nonsense, so that funds will be quickly allocated to this troubled city."[15]

Shriver could not have agreed more about the crucial role the lack of a poverty agency played in the Watts revolt. He placed the blame squarely on the shoulders of local officials, especially Yorty. In a memo to White House press secretary Bill Moyers written a week after the beginning of the revolt, Shriver noted that local officials had resisted the expansion of its CAA into a broadly representative body. He later told the *Los Angeles Times* that Los Angeles was the only major city without a major CAA "because of the failure of local officials."[16]

In response, Yorty turned around and blamed Shriver and OEO. In one of his typically self-serving letters, Yorty wrote George Murphy: "One of the riot inciting factors is the deliberate and well publicized cutting off of poverty funds to this city pending our efforts to reorganize the Youth Opportunities Board to meet the chameleonic OEO criteria. Other cities have not been subjected to such strong arm tactics. . . . There has been a reckless effort to incite the poor for political purposes. . . . Please demand that Shriver process our program and release our funds while we reorganize. . . . If funds are not provided at once for our program I should like to suggest a Senate inquiry."[17]

Following these accusations, Shriver claimed that Yorty had turned down an offer of funds before the revolt. He noted that OEO had sent $17 million to EYOA, despite the fact that Los Angeles had not complied with OEO's representational prerequisites. In a letter to Murphy, Shriver explained that OEO had not sent more money because minority groups and the poor would not be represented adequately on EYOA's board.[18] Years later the bitterness remained. In an oral history interview, Yorty contended that accusations claiming he had failed to cooperate in the formation of EYOA were "the effort that the left wing made, to make it appear that it was my fault."[19] One thing Yorty and Shriver could agree on—the disagreement over the poverty program had played a significant role in the anger and frustration that led to the Watts revolt.

Residents of the area and participants in the revolt saw a direct connection between the antipoverty stalemate and the revolt. A much higher rate of people arrested in the Watts violence disapproved of EYOA than did people in the general black population in Los Angeles.[20] J. Stanley Sanders, a Watts native and an attorney and leader in Watts during the post-revolt era, has argued that "the prominent issue" that led to the Watts revolt "was the holdup of poverty funds. . . . There was a lot of dissension and ill will on account of that."[21] Father Morris Samuel, known as Father Sam, a white Episcopal priest serving in

South Central who worked at the Westminster Neighborhood Association and was an active member of the local chapter of CORE, put the attitude of many of the revolt participants bluntly: "We've been asking, pleading for better housing, better facilities and by burning these buildings down we can show Mayor Yorty and his friends that they can't sit on that anti-poverty money and not let us have it."[22]

Additional evidence that government officials connected Watts to the antipoverty fiasco was the infusion of money and antipoverty programs that entered Los Angeles in the days, weeks, and months that followed. In an August 23 memo to Joe Califano on what OEO could do to aid riot areas, Shriver noted that they could approve grants of $2.5 million for remedial education, legal services, and a small business-development center. The government task forces and commissions made similar recommendations. The McCone Commission suggested an increase in OEO funds for employment and job- training programs, as well as money for preschool education. The President's Task Force on the Los Angeles Riots recommended forty-nine projects, many of them OEO-funded, which were needed in Los Angeles. They included more Youth Opportunity Centers, legal services, full implementation of Head Start, a number of education-related projects, and improved community participation in Community Action Programs (CAPs).[23]

OEO responded quickly to the recommendations, making an additional $2.2 million available for work-training programs by early September. That money helped fund 1,200 jobs through the Neighborhood Youth Corps (NYC). By mid-October OEO had sent over $7 million for various EYOA projects, including Teen Post programs, food stamps, vocational rehabilitation, and job training.[24]

The Watts revolt also led to a white backlash. The Report of the President's Task Force noted that "the prevalent attitude in the white community is to condemn the lawlessness." The white population in California after Watts was "far less sympathetic to . . . the needs of the poverty areas than before the riots. . . . Many see a close connection between peaceful demonstrations for civil rights and the rioting." White resistance to African American civil rights and participation in the War on Poverty provided stark evidence of the pervasiveness of America's "racial nationalism."[25]

Watts influenced the course of the civil rights movement and demonstrated the class divisions within the African American community. The middle-class, southern civil rights movement, focused on voting rights and desegregating public facilities, seemed to have little pertinence for blacks in Los Angeles. African Americans in Los Angeles could vote and ride on buses and eat at lunch counters. Some working-class African Americans in Los Angeles identified more closely with the separatist philosophy of Malcolm X and the Nation of Islam (NOI) and their message of economic power than with the integrationist ideology of Martin Luther King, Jr., and the Southern Christian Leadership Conference (SCLC). For those blacks who adhered to the ideology of black nationalism in its various forms, America was a completely racialized nation that was corrupt to the core and would never welcome blacks as equals.[26]

In fact, Malcolm X and the NOI had made significant inroads among blacks in Los Angeles after 1962, when they aggressively and openly supported a group of black Muslims from Los Angeles accused of shooting police officers in a case that reeked of police brutality. During his stay in Los Angeles, Malcolm X "captivated mass meetings from the floor of prestigious Christian churches with electrifying oratory about Chief Parker's force as a daily oppression for Negroes." From that point on, the black Muslim presence in Los Angeles increased significantly. Malcolm X's assassination in February 1965 and the posthumous publication of his autobiography in October of that year, two months after the Watts revolt, furthered the popularity of his ideology of black nationalism, particularly among young, urban blacks in Los Angeles and nationally. Indeed, a 1967 survey of Watts residents found that nearly 60 percent supported the ideas of black nationalism, while only 24 percent opposed it.[27]

Some of the growth of the NOI in Los Angeles was based on class differences, real or perceived. Some blacks in Watts felt middle-class African Americans, who were more likely to be lighter in skin color, looked down on them as poor and dark skinned. The Nation of Islam was able to draw some of these blacks away from traditional Christian churches, because they "had failed to attend to the temporal needs of many of its parishioners." One participant in the Watts revolt who had joined the Nation of Islam disdained the middle-class leaders in Los Angeles's black community as not "worth anything" and asserted that they did not "care about poor people." On August 15, 1965, Marquette Frye, one of the brothers arrested in the incident that sparked the violence, spoke at a gathering of black Muslims in Los Angeles and argued that the violence in Watts was a manifestation of the teachings of Elijah Muhammad. Social scientist Paul Bullock interviewed young people in Watts after the violence and found that the youths greatly admired Malcolm X but were ambiguous about King. They did not trust King because he was a minister, and they did not accept non-violence as a philosophy. In addition, Bullock noted hearing phrases such as "Black Awareness" and "Black Pride" more frequently after Watts. He also observed that young blacks "demand greater control over the institutions in their community, and a more meaningful voice in the decisions that govern the present and shape their future." Watts, indeed, "marked a shift toward nationalism and away from integration, toward racial conservatism and away from liberalism." And both the Watts revolt and black nationalism would further the resistance of some African Americans to a city-controlled War on Poverty.[28]

Others also recognized the class and ideological differences within the black community. The Report of the President's Task Force noted that "for most Negroes in Los Angeles the traditional goals of the civil rights movement have not been particularly germane."[29] Political activist Saul Alinsky argued that civil rights leaders were "out of touch with the masses and the gut issues."[30] One resident of Watts told a reporter: "the ministers have lost contact with us, and the politicians only want to use us. There's nobody really gives a damn about us."[31] A civil rights worker argued that the movement had "failed in Watts. . . . It wasn't political here. It was economic and social and in the end beyond us."[32] California state assemblyman Mervyn Dymally, who represented South Central Los Angeles, admitted that Watts constituted in part "a revolt against the Negro leadership."[33] In the immediate aftermath of the Watts revolt, the *New Republic* editorialized, "The civil rights movement in Los Angeles has been middle class. It never found a way to reach or enlist the masses in the ghetto. It has been concerned with business and professional-class Negroes who want to move to all-white neighborhoods."[34]

Martin Luther King, Jr., the most widely recognized leader of the civil rights movement in the South, returned to Los Angeles a week after the violence to meet with local leaders, black and white. King decided to visit Watts after seeing television footage of evangelist Billy Graham flying over the riot area in a helicopter with Mayor Yorty. King met with Rev. Thomas Kilgore, the head of the Los Angeles chapter of the SCLC; Norman Houston, president of the L.A. chapter of the NAACP; and Brookins. He also called on the city to increase the representation of the poor and minorities on the antipoverty board. The experience jolted King and influenced his perception of civil rights and poverty.[35]

This was not the first time King had been to L.A.; indeed, he had made several trips to Los Angeles prior to his visit in July 1965. In 1961 King headlined a rally at the Sports Arena that attracted forty thousand. The following year, in June 1962, he made appearances at several churches in Los Angeles, as well as at a rally at the University of Southern California (USC), where he spoke on "Powers Greater Than Violence." During that visit King was hailed by Governor Brown, County Supervisor Kenneth Hahn, and Mayor Yorty as "a crusader for the cause of . . . freedom." One year later, on May 26, 1963, King spoke at a "Rally for Freedom" at Wrigley Field in Los Angeles in support of the Birmingham movement. The Reverend H. H. Brookins served as master of ceremonies for the event, and the Reverend E. V. Hill gave the offertory prayer, so the ministers who later battled over the War on Poverty in 1963 were united in support of King. Celebrities Dick Gregory, Dorothy Dandridge, Rita Moreno, Paul Newman, and Joanne Woodward also appeared to fete King and provide financial support for the movement. Mayor Yorty had met King at the airport and presented him with a key to the city. During King's visit earlier in 1965, perhaps his most celebrated, he was honored at a banquet sponsored by the city of Los Angeles. The highlight of the evening, outside of King's speech, was Mayor Yorty's welcome. Yorty told the crowd, "It is a great honor that this great Nobel Peace Prize winner has come to our city." Yorty presented King with a plaque and declared it "Martin Luther King Day" in Los Angeles, telling King, "We would like you to know that the welcome mat is always out for you." The welcome mat was not so visible five months later.[36]

When he returned to Los Angeles in August 1965, King attended a community gathering at the Westminster Neighborhood Association in Watts to discuss the area's problems and some possible solutions. For the first time in his life, he was booed and heckled by a black audience. One man yelled, " 'Get out of here, Dr. King! We don't want you.' " This response demonstrated an outright rejection of King's primary strategy of nonviolent direct-action protest aimed at social equality. For some in the audience that day, that message did not seem germane to their reality. When he started a speech with "All over America the Negroes must join hands," one person in the audience interrupted, "and burn." While King was the recipient of much of the anger that day, the audience made it clear that the real targets of their vitriol were Yorty and Parker. One woman told King, "Let Parker and Yorty come down here and see how we're doing." A teenage girl added, "And they will burn the most!" Although the shouting died down enough for King to give a speech and hold a question-and-answer period with the audience, their overall reception of King and his message was mixed.[37]

King's nearly three-hour conference with Yorty and Parker was even less successful. Both the mayor and the police chief "steadfastly denied the existence of prejudice anywhere in Los Angeles." King was unable to persuade Yorty to make any movement on the antipoverty board issue, and he left the discussion viewing Yorty as stubborn and inept. After the meeting, Yorty blasted King for criticizing the police department, hinted that King had communist connections, and called the reverend's visit "a great disservice to the people of Los Angeles and to the nation."[38]

In addition to those encounters, King toured South Central, viewed the devastation, and talked to people about their problems. What he saw and heard informed his already developing perspective of the fundamental need for economic justice. He admitted to reporters a "growing disillusionment and resentment toward the Negro middle class and the leadership it has produced" and said that "we as Negro leaders—and I include myself—have failed to take the civil rights movement to the masses of the people."[39] Presidential assistant Lee White reported that King "views Los Angeles as basically an economic conflict between the haves and the have-nots, definitely not a racial dispute."[40]

President Johnson talked to the civil rights leader on August 20 to get King's impressions of the situation. They agreed that Yorty was a stumbling block, LBJ telling King that Yorty "opposed even limited poverty funds unless he controlled them." King intimated that he saw the antipoverty stalemate as critical, telling the president that starting a War on Poverty in Los Angeles "in the next few days . . . would help a great deal." LBJ told King, "we'll get at it" and then told his staff, "let's get up a program."[41]

Bayard Rustin accompanied King to Los Angeles and noted the influence his visit to Watts had had on the reverend's thinking. King told Rustin that visiting Watts had made clear to him the "material and spiritual desolation" of blacks in America's inner cities. While King's message had always included economic justice, it became a central part of his thinking and message after Watts.[42]

Viewing the devastation firsthand and facing the criticism that civil rights leaders had failed to reach out to urban blacks "depressed" King and led him to action. He wanted to prove that nonviolence could work outside of the South. In late August 1965, King called an emergency meeting of the SCLC executive staff. A few days later he and the SCLC officially shifted their efforts from south to north and from desegregation and voting rights to economic issues, such as housing discrimination in Chicago. Watts had served as the catalyst that convinced King to initiate a northern campaign focusing on economic issues. Thus, the Watts revolt and the War on Poverty fiasco in Los Angeles made key contributions in leading civil rights leaders to address publicly issues of economic justice in America.[43] Watts directly connected the War on Poverty and the civil rights movement; what remained to be seen was the effect Watts would have on the War on Poverty in Los Angeles.

"The air was more filled with tension than smog"

Perhaps the greatest indicator of the significance of the stalled community-action program to the Watts revolt was the haste with which the administration attempted to solve the dilemma. Initially, LBJ refused to accept that Watts had happened. Only five days before the revolt, he had signed the Voting Rights Act, which many Americans, black and white, saw as the culmination of the civil rights movement. When Johnson first heard the news from Watts, "he just couldn't accept it. He refused to look at the cable from Los Angeles describing the situation. . . . he simply wouldn't respond."[44] On August 14 Johnson finally broke his silence and discussed the situation in Watts with Joseph Califano, special assistant to the president. The president was concerned over the effect the revolt would have on white Americans and depressed to think that the violence would create irreparable damage to his Great Society. He also wanted Americans to understand the plight of Watts's residents.[45]

The normally restless Johnson's period of inactivity did not last long. On August 17 the president dispatched LeRoy Collins, his director of the new Community Relations Service (the agency within the Commerce Department that dealt with civil rights issues), to Los Angeles to help resolve the difficulties arising from the revolt. Collins, the former governor of Florida, had earlier in the year negotiated the compromise with King that led King to turn the marchers around on the Edmund Pettus Bridge outside of Selma. Collins stayed until the twenty-fourth, after his return filing a comprehensive report that outlined his experience in Los Angeles.[46]

When Collins arrived in Los Angeles on Wednesday, August 18, "the air was more filled with tension than smog." Collins noted immediately that everyone was pointing fingers at others; no clear leadership had emerged. He realized after his first day in Los Angeles that "no general progress could be made toward restoring calm in that city until the anti-poverty squabble was resolved. Mayor Yorty and Sargent Shriver continued to swap transcontinental insults; the Governor was gigging the Mayor about being a dog in the manger regarding the anti-poverty program; the two Congressmen [Hawkins and Roybal] were prodding Shriver to get tougher on the Mayor, and a militant group of Negroes in the Watts area was lambasting Negro Councilman Billy Mills for 'selling out' to the Mayor."[47]

Despite these political hurdles, Collins initially was able to make some progress on settling the EYOA dispute. The key issue remained representation of the poor. Collins persuaded city and county officials to agree with Reverend Brookins that the American Arbitration Association could determine the methods by which representatives of the poor would be elected. He also realized, however, that arbitration would take too much time. Interim representatives of the poor would have to be chosen in order to get the EYOA running immediately. In his negotiations to determine how to choose those interim representatives, Collins kept encountering stumbling blocks. Upon investigation, he discovered that the person holding up the process was Jesse Unruh, a political rival of Governor Brown's and a sometime friend of Yorty's. Yorty had delegated his negotiation responsibilities to Billy Mills. Collins discovered that Mills's deputy, Willard Murray, was a political cohort of Unruh's—Mills was taking his direction from Murray, who was taking his from Unruh. Collins wrote LBJ that "it was upon Murray that every possibility of compromise seemed to hang up."[48]

Resourceful in his determination to solve the gridlock, Collins contacted Carman Warschaw, a California member of the Democratic National Committee and chair of the California Fair Employment Practices Commission, and persuaded her to discuss the situation with Unruh. The following day, Unruh suddenly expressed the need to meet with Collins. Collins outlined the situation to Unruh, and within one hour, Mills and Yorty were ready to compromise and settle the issue. Mills had received criticism from his district for his previous support of Yorty's proposal and was ready to support the compromise. Collins colorfully noted that "once Councilman Mills was turned around, Mayor Yorty had no reason—or excuse—to remain adamant. He would have been recognized, and condemned, by all as a dog in the manger."[49]

The agreement they reached included the following points: EYOA would consist of a twenty-five-member board, including twelve public-agency members, seven community representatives "selected by a democratic process," six private-agency representatives (United Way, AFL-CIO, etc.), and two nonvoting members (Los Angeles Chamber of Commerce and League of California Cities); the election process was to be determined by the American Arbitration Association; and four community representatives would be appointed until the elections were held. Collins wired the details of the agreement to Shriver on August 23; later that day, Shriver wired back that the agreement met with OEO approval.[50]

The settlement did not, however, meet with resounding applause from many African Americans. Brookins initially told the press that the plan was acceptable, "which got him into all kinds of hot water with his people in the Watts area." The membership of the CAPC was initially critical of the compromise in part because Collins had not consulted with the poor before making the agreement. According to U.S. Attorney General Ramsey Clark, the CAPC members "were furious. They were unhappy with the agreement, unhappy with their lack of involvement in details of negotiations . . . and unhappy with Brookins's statement and weak negotiating role." The CAPC members believed they had been sold out—it had been demanded that they be represented on the board, but they had not been consulted before the compromise was agreed upon. As a result, Lewis Green, a CAPC member and the chair of United Neighborhood Organizations in Watts, warned that Watts's residents would "go to the streets to demonstrate and protest" against the Collins compromise. Many in CAPC saw these developments as further evidence of the failure of middle-class leadership. Green noted that he respected Brookins, Norman Houston, H. Claude Hudson, and the other middle-class blacks who agreed to Collins's compromise, "but I don't want them representing Watts, because they don't come from Watts." Tony Tinajero and Anthony Rios, Mexican American members of CAPC, expressed "immediate distrust" of the Mexican Americans included on the EYOA board, whom they saw as being "far removed from any contact or identification with the bulk of the poor" in East Los Angeles. Brookins considered resigning from CAPC, but Collins convinced him to stay.[51]

Congressman Hawkins was initially unhappy with the plan, in part because of CAPC's anger and also because he had developed a plan to present to Shriver himself but had not yet been able to present his proposal. Hawkins blasted the agreement because it was made without community input, but after talking to Collins and getting him to agree to meet with people in the black neighborhoods, Hawkins promised to cooperate.[52]

Despite his eventual agreement with the Collins compromise, Yorty did not fare well in Collins's assessment. Collins claimed that Yorty had issued statements to the press that Collins's presence could not serve any purpose in Los Angeles. Collins reported to LBJ that he "found the Mayor a most difficult man. Perhaps it is because he accurately reflects the confusing condition of Los Angeles and its people. In any event, he is harder to work with than a tomato seed on a wet plate."[53] On the other hand, Collins had high praise for Brookins. He noted that despite all the negatives he had heard about Brookins from Yorty and his colleagues, he found Brookins "to be a calm and reliable voice of reason. I would hate to see him ground under."[54]

On his last night in Los Angeles, after the agreement had already been reached, Collins, at the request of Hawkins and Brookins, attended a community meeting in Watts to discuss the antipoverty settlement. Many in the group belonged to CAPC and were angered by not being included in the decision-making process. Collins regretted not meeting with them sooner and realized the importance of participation to the people of Watts.

I should have gone straight out to the Watts area and listened and let the people know that someone . . . wanted to know what was hurting them and cared about them. . . . by then it was a little late. For nearly two hours I met with a large number of those people in the Watts area while they tore my hide off, pouring out all the fury of their resentment against the white man and his officials. . . . They were just telling me how they felt—mostly about the Mayor and the Chief of Police and some of the Negro politicians who work with the city officials. If I had endured this experience early in the mission, I would have been better equipped to answer some of the local officials' adamant contentions that they alone are properly able to represent the poor.[55]

Thus, issues of race, class, and political power (representation of the poor) remained significant to the residents of Watts.

The experience made Collins realize the importance of participation to the people in Watts. He knew if that was not achieved, the EYOA troubles would continue; consequently, he ended his report in an ominous tone, which Johnson "brooded over for weeks."[56]

Although the rioting has ended, the underlying causes remain. The poverty program will help get at these causes. . . . But the biggest and most dangerous ingredient is a feeling on the part of the Negro community in Los Angeles that they are "out of it." They will continue to risk riots, in my opinion, until some means are found for giving those people a genuine sense of participation in the affairs of the community at large. . . . I have an uneasy feeling that things are far from settled in Los Angeles. While we reached an agreement which made it possible to get the anti-poverty program off the ground, the struggle over who is to represent the poor in that program will, in my opinion, continue. [57]

Collins was right in his assessment of the situation. Lack of participation and the need for a sense of control over their own lives resonated with the residents of South Central Los Angeles. Many had also been profoundly affected by the cultural, political, and economic empowerment tenets of Malcolm X and the Nation of Islam. And they believed their attempts to gain political power had been thwarted by the EYOA compromise. Many African Americans were not ready to unite behind EYOA—self determination and empowerment mattered.

How well did the agreement address issues of representation and participation? Unruh, speaker of the California State Assembly, told Johnson he was "satisfied that the new 25-man board will not only provide good poverty community representation, but will essentially prevent the establishment of personal political machines."[58] Of course, Unruh was a political friend of Yorty's. This may help explain his exuberance for an agreement that would still allow public-agency control of EYOA. A different assessment of the compromise came from the *New Republic*. In a September 1965 editorial, the magazine claimed that LBJ had given Yorty $20 million in poverty funds "to maintain Los Angeles's Negro colonies as the Mayor sees fit. . . . It seems unlikely that the Los Angeles poverty program will ever reflect any other aspirations than those of Yorty. The people to be affected once again will not have any say in what happens to them."[59]

The *New Republic* may have overstated LBJ's intentions. The administration did offer the $20 million in poverty funds in the hopes that it would settle the rioters, but it also took steps to keep Yorty from complete control of EYOA. Yorty and his backers had prevailed in maintaining public-agency dominance in voting power, but supporters of increased power to the communities had also won a victory, since community representatives would be elected by the poor. For those in the black community who had hoped for more community control over the agency, however, the compromise was understandably disappointing. The agreement, while impinging somewhat on Yorty's dominance, still gave the mayor the upper hand in the struggle over EYOA. That further increased some African Americans' disenchantment with the EYOA.

A Divided Black Leadership

Class, political, and ideological divisions also inhibited African Americans' willingness to support the EYOA. After the EYOA settlement, African American leaders each had their own following, and they were reluctant to work together. Black ministers remained hopelessly divided over the EYOA compromise. Community leaders could not agree on whom to support in the 1965 mayoral election. Hawkins and Bradley were the only major black politicians to support the liberal James Roosevelt. Mills, Lindsay, and others supported Yorty, despite his continued alliance with Chief Parker. Yorty had supported Mills's and Lindsay's campaigns, and in that sense, they owed the mayor. Mills had also served as Yorty's negotiator during the EYOA deliberations.[60]

Yorty contributed to some of the political divisions within the black community. On April 18, 1966, in an apparent attempt by Yorty to keep the black community divided, Councilman Mills resigned from the board of EYOA, stating that he was resigning because the War on Poverty had promised more than it could deliver. He charged Shriver and OEO with refusing to cooperate in solving the problems of the poor, problems that Mills claimed had been created by OEO itself. In a stunning indictment of himself and other city leaders, Mills argued, "we have gone from crisis to crisis merely to leave the people for whose benefit the program was intended hurt, angry and confused, with the guilty on both sides pointing to the other, pretending to be concerned about the poor while actually using their plight as a platform for selfishly motivated attacks and counterattacks."[61]

Mills, who represented largely working-class and unemployed

blacks, did seem legitimately concerned about the lack of jobs included in the War on Poverty. In blaming others, however, he was doing just what he accused other local leaders of doing—pointing fingers and not seriously addressing the problem. As Yorty's right-hand man in the EYOA negotiations, Mills was more responsible for the stalled negotiations than anyone but Yorty himself.

To replace Mills on the EYOA board, Yorty chose Edward Hawkins, older brother of congressman Gus Hawkins, Yorty's longtime political foe. Yorty apparently made the appointment to needle the congressman. Edward Hawkins had previously been on the Board of Public Works and had no experience related to the War on Poverty. Mills argued that the appointment of Hawkins to succeed him was a brilliant move that would lead to "a reconciliation between the two antagonists in the local poverty program—Congressman Hawkins and the mayor."[62]

Mills knew better. He knew, as did most political observers in Los Angeles, that the Hawkins brothers' relationship was troubled. The problems had begun in 1962, when Gus ran for Congress and Ed ran for the State Assembly seat Gus was vacating. Gus refused to back Ed, because he believed his older brother viewed politics as a business. When Ed lost, Yorty seized an opportunity and immediately took him under his wing, appointing him to the Board of Public Works.[63]

Ed Hawkins had sided with Yorty in the EYOA battles long before his appointment to the board. In an August 6 telegram to Gus, Ed told his brother, "your so-called hearing and investigation into the antipoverty program, over which you have the audacity to act as investigator, judge and jury, is a farce."[64] Yorty's appointment of Ed Hawkins was not an attempt to repair the rift and bring peace to EYOA. Rather, it represented an attempt to keep the black community divided and help Yorty maintain his political power.

Congressman Hawkins's response was not surprising. He questioned his brother's knowledge and experience and accused Yorty of "playing games" and seeking to strengthen his position in the black community, as well as maintaining his control over EYOA funds. Ed knocked Gus for attacking Yorty and accused his brother of damaging "the harmonious functioning of [EYOA]."[65] These brotherly spats and the internecine warfare, which did nothing to aid the progress and success of EYOA, continued until August of 1967, when Ed Hawkins resigned from the EYOA board. Yorty replaced Hawkins with Willard Murray, the man who—along with Mills—had helped to hold up an agreement in the aftermath of Watts.[66]

The Hawkins brothers' clash was only one of many signs of trouble for EYOA in 1966. In January Gus Hawkins wrote President Johnson that the EYOA's handling of antipoverty funds could "provoke further disorders and violence unless checked."[67] In February an OEO Office of Inspection team visited EYOA and described the situation in Los Angeles as "extremely serious."[68] Samuel Yette believed that OEO was "facing a new crisis in Los Angeles," while another OEO staffer noted that "while EYOA goes through the political gymnastics, the town seethes in conflict and chaos."[69]

In addition to slowing the chances of success for EYOA, the Hawkins rift symbolized part of the larger general problems of divided black leadership, political bickering, and class divisions. Bradley, Mills, Brookins, and the two Hawkins all suffered from, and contributed to, divisions within the black community in part because of an inability to overcome concern for their own political livelihood. While Brookins and Gus Hawkins made legitimate attempts to make EYOA representative of the poor, neither was able to do it.

Nothing demonstrated the divisions within the black community better than the Watts revolt. A direct attack not only against mainstream white society, but also against middle-class black leadership, Watts demonstrated that the civil rights gains in the South would not solve the problems in the major cities of the North and West. Watts increased divisions within the black community in Los Angeles and the civil rights community at large, and it was one of the key factors (along with the Vietnam War) that helped unravel the Johnson presidency. Watts also encouraged blacks in many cities, including Los Angeles, to use the community-action structure of the War on Poverty to make economic demands. Unfortunately, political and class divisions within the black community hampered their ability to unite behind the War on Poverty and thwarted the success of EYOA.

Another reason for the failure of blacks to gain political power through EYOA was Mayor Yorty. His egocentrism never served him worse than in the EYOA disputes. Unwilling to compromise unless backed to the wall, even then he refused to cooperate and instead initiated his own brand of guerrilla warfare against community representation in EYOA and the War on Poverty. Yorty's divisive personality and actions helped further divide the people of Los Angeles. Thus, issues of race, class, and political power stymied the ability of the African American poor to gain a sense of political power and control over their own lives through EYOA.

Chapter 3
Interracial Strife and the
Neighborhood Adult Participation Project

WEAKENED BY DIVISIONS AMONG African Americans and political battles between city hall and community representatives, EYOA provided
services to some of the poor amidst considerable turmoil. What provoked much of the conflict in EYOA in the mid- to late 1960s was
interracial strife between Mexican Americans and African Americans
over one particular EYOA program—the Neighborhood Adult Participation Project (NAPP). NAPP was the only EYOA program actually
involved in community action and organization. It was one of the few
programs directed by a woman, Opal Jones, and consisted of mostly
female employees. As such, it presaged the number of community
antipoverty organizations nationwide in the late 1960s and early 1970s
that would be dominated by women. Under the auspices of the YOB
and the Los Angeles Area Federation of Settlements and Neighborhood Centers (LAAFSNC), NAPP, which opened its doors at its headquarters in an office at the old Wrigley Field baseball stadium on April
1, 1965, was one of the few War on Poverty programs in Los Angeles to
begin before the Watts revolt. The YOB initially proposed NAPP to
OEO in November 1964 as an employment and on-the-job training
program. Despite her opposition to EYOA and because of her work at the
Avalon Community Center, YOB staff recruited Jones to head NAPP.
The centrality of community organization convinced Jones to head
NAPP. Her position of leadership as a woman of color made Jones the
center of two significant controversies—participation of the poor and
racial strife between blacks and Mexican Americans. In December, during meetings between Jones and a representative from the President's
Task Force on the War on Poverty, the concept of community-service
centers, or outposts, which would focus more on community organization
than employment, became a central goal of the new agency.[1]

NAPP consisted of thirteen outposts, with one outpost located in each of thirteen poverty areas identified by the Los Angeles Welfare Planning Council. Each of the outposts employed thirty workers, or aides. NAPP aides were poor and unemployed residents who lived in the community in which they worked. Jones referred to NAPP aides as "change agents," because they would not only be employed by public or private agencies, but would also change the agency's traditional methods. Jones admitted that the notion of change agents was "frightening to the agencies," but, as she explained, NAPP was "only trying to bring them in closer touch with the grass roots." Some of those change agents served in schools as teacher aides and registered people for Head Start, others served as liaisons between the public and various government agencies, while three employees at each outpost worked as information aides. These aides went door to door in each neighborhood asking families what their needs were, what they would like to see in the neighborhood, and how community members could work together to accomplish them. In its early existence, NAPP succeeded in organizing neighborhoods for better street lighting, weekly garbage collection, child-care homes, and food reserves. NAPP also provided adult education classes, conducted voter-registration drives, and aided the unemployed in finding jobs. Thus, NAPP used a "double-edged approach" to fighting poverty—job training and placement and community action. NAPP's Annual Report for 1966 featured a cartoon with a baby (NAPP) struggling under a large sack (titled "heavy load") filled with a number of the agency's programs and responsibilities. In the middle of the sack, as it was at the center of NAPP, was citizen participation.[2]

But NAPP's community organization angered some of the local government agencies and the mayor. The first signs of trouble over NAPP came in January 1966, when councilman Tom Bradley telephoned Samuel Yette, an OEO official, and complained that Mayor Yorty was trying to take over NAPP by gerrymandering the city for the EYOA board election. Yorty was making another attempt to maintain control and political power over EYOA. He saw NAPP as a political threat and took action. According to Yette, "Bradley felt that this move could be catalytic."[3]

OEO discussed the possibility of dismantling EYOA into several

Opal Jones and city councilman Tom Bradley (right) with an unidentified man outside the Avalon Community Center in December 1962. Jones was executive director and Bradley was president of the community center prior to Jones's becoming director of NAPP. The center became one of the NAPP outposts under Jones's direction. Bradley remained an ardent supporter of Jones throughout her involvement with NAPP and the War on Poverty. Courtesy Los Angeles Public Library.

smaller agencies, since EYOA was experiencing many political and administrative problems. OEO considered various methods to reduce EYOA's scope, including divesting it of its NAPP operations and creating Neighborhood Councils to bring the War on Poverty more directly to the people. When OEO staff broached these ideas to Congressman Hawkins, he heartily endorsed them, hoping to dissolve EYOA, or at least reduce its scope, and to allow other CAAs to fill the void. He also agreed with the idea of divesting EYOA of its NAPP responsibilities. According to Hawkins, NAPP was not organizing communities as well as it could, because EYOA was throwing stumbling blocks at it. Hawkins may have had another motive. Jones was known to be a "close political ally" of Hawkins and had undoubtedly been targeted by Yorty in part because of that connection.[4]

The issue came to a head in April 1966. On April 1 Jones penned an angry nine-page letter to EYOA executive director Joe Maldonado (a Mexican American who had previously been a social worker), complaining about EYOA's attempt to shift NAPP from community organization to job training and placement. In her letter Jones argued that EYOA "always seemed to be on the side of the powerful." She also lamented that she had been "ordered to stay away from the community and civil rights meetings as they struggled to have a part in the formation of an anti-poverty group in Los Angeles." Her letter certainly added to the growing tension between EYOA and NAPP. In the first few days of the month, as rumors continued to circulate about NAPP and EYOA, Jones and her colleagues called a meeting of NAPP participants to criticize EYOA, clarify the role NAPP should play in the War on Poverty, and discuss troubled relations between African Americans and Mexican Americans in her organization. Maldonado learned of the meeting and ordered Jones to call it off. She refused and held the meeting, and on April 4 Maldonado fired her for insubordination.[5] Jones believed she was fired both because of her support of citizen participation and because she was a woman. She told the *Sentinel,* "I will fight for my own right and reputation as a social worker and for NAPP to become an independent, vital community action program." She argued that Maldonado should interact with her "not only as a woman, but as a staff member." The firing touched off a storm of protest. Over three hundred people, mostly blacks and Latinos, congregated in the Wrigley Field parking lot outside of NAPP headquarters. Led by Congressman Hawkins, they protested Jones's firing and blamed Yorty. Another group led a march to picket the EYOA offices.[6]

Jones's firing also created turmoil within the EYOA board. Initially, a confused board upheld her firing, but after she appealed the decision, all the community representatives changed their minds. In fact, four of them participated in the rally to protest Jones's firing. While the board at its meeting gave Maldonado a vote of confidence, the vote was not unanimous—most of the community representatives voted against the EYOA director.[7]

In the midst of the maelstrom, OEO needed to create a plan to handle the crisis. On April 7, after discussions with OEO leadership in Washington, Daniel Luevano issued a directive divesting EYOA from direct control over NAPP. The Los Angeles Area Federation of Settlements would have direct control over NAPP. In addition, OEO proceeded to organize Neighborhood Councils with powers to initiate and approve programs for their areas. Finally, the regional office would consider applications for the funding of independent CAAs in areas with populations of one hundred thousand or more.[8]

Reaction to the OEO directive was decidedly mixed. Spokespersons for the black community generally viewed it positively. Brookins hailed the directive as "a first step in bringing the poverty program back to the people."[9] The Los Angeles Sentinel applauded the decision and showed its wholehearted support for NAPP. According to the Sentinel, "the major community thrust in Los Angeles has been NAPP and its successful operation has been a threat to the power structure of EYOA. Contrary to the will of EYOA, NAPP has operated a true community action program concerned with giving the poor themselves a voice in a program theoretically designed to aid them."[10] Opal Jones had made NAPP focus on community participation and forced EYOA's divestment of its control of NAPP. NAPP would now have some independence, guided by the LAAFSNC instead of EYOA. Jones's future, though, remained undetermined.

Other black leaders did not respond so favorably to divestment. In his resignation letter from the EYOA board, Billy Mills blasted the directive, projecting that it would cause a return to "the old practice of employing only those who are known or friendly to a director or administrator of a given project." Mills went on to predict that Los Angeles could "expect the poverty program to degenerate into the most cruel federal patronage vehicle in recent history." Not surprisingly, Mills's replacement on the board, Willard Murray, harbored the same opposition to the directive.[11]

The Los Angeles Sentinel saw through Mills's resignation. According to the Sentinel, "in addition to fostering Yorty's opportunism and serving as a 'swan song,' Mills's resignation was also a fast moving vehicle to head off Shriver and the divestment of EYOA." The paper was right in noting that while Mills claimed to be "frustrated by the confusion of the poverty program," he knew exactly what he was doing in resigning.[12]

OEO's directive angered the mayor. On April 11 Yorty wrote to LBJ complaining about the decision and the fact that OEO informed him only a few minutes before the directive was released to the press. He snapped: "I am becoming increasingly provoked with the arrogant attitude of the Office of Economic Opportunity toward my administration and the lack of even ordinary courtesy."[13]

Two weeks later he fired off another missive to Johnson. Yorty claimed divestment would result in a scramble to create CAAs, would increase EYOA costs, and threatened that he might attempt to thwart the implementation of the local Head Start programs if the divestment proceeded. Then he resorted once again to complaining and blaming others:

It is clear now that the poverty program in Los Angeles is in danger of collapsing. We have reached this critical state because of ill-considered actions taken by the Office of Economic Opportunity and because there has been a deliberate attempt to sabotage the program on the part of some federal officials who, for their own political gain, are attaching my name to every failure and every controversy which arises in the administration of the program. Congressman Hawkins . . . is continuously misleading the community by stating that I run the program and that I am preventing the poor from realizing its benefits.[14]

Faced with opposition, Yorty once more could do no better than point fingers.

In addition to irritating the mayor, Luevano's directive created some confusion among the EYOA board members. They postponed a public hearing on the firing of Opal Jones, because they needed to clarify NAPP's status following the divestment order. The meeting was rescheduled for several days later. When the board finally met, Maldonado told them that Jones had solicited funds to make an unauthorized trip to Washington, D.C., in order to convince OEO to divest NAPP from EYOA. Jones admitted that she had made the trip to plead her case with OEO, but claimed she took the trip on her own vacation time and at her own expense. She also noted that some staff members gave her money to help defray costs.[15]

The *Los Angeles Sentinel* insightfully noted that "the real and recurring issue between Mrs. Jones and the EYOA is in the philosophy behind the operation of her NAPP program." According to the newspaper's assessment, NAPP could continue to be successful only if it was "taken completely from under the political thumb of the EYOA and . . . Mayor Yorty and his men Robert Goe, [and] Maldonado."[16] The real issue was political power.

Both sides in the controversy appealed to OEO and the Johnson administration for intervention. Shriver used his political skills to get Yorty and Maldonado to agree to rehire Jones as long NAPP was divested from EYOA. By removing NAPP from EYOA's direct control, neither Maldonado nor Yorty would be responsible for Jones's activities. What had seemed appalling to Yorty and Maldonado now seemed reasonable, and the issue was to be finalized at an April 25 EYOA board meeting.[17]

The meeting did not proceed as planned, however. After vehement arguments, the seven poverty-area representatives and Yorty's representative voted for Jones's reinstatement, while every other member (twelve total) voted against it. Maldonado was not dissuaded. Immediately after the meeting, he rehired Jones to NAPP on a temporary basis, for the remaining time of EYOA's control over it. Operational control of NAPP would be turned over to the Federation of Settlements in July, while policy coordination would remain in the hands of EYOA. For one of the few times in EYOA's history, the poverty representatives and the city were in agreement.[18] Opal Jones had wrenched control of NAPP from Mayor Yorty and the EYOA and placed it in her hands and the hands of her "change agents."

While the issue of representation was temporarily resolved, NAPP remained a center of controversy. Key to its presence in the eye of the War on Poverty storm in Los Angeles was interracial antagonism. From the beginning, Mexican Americans questioned NAPP's racial configuration. Of the thirteen outposts, only three, those in East Los Angeles, Boyle Heights, and Pacoima, were in Mexican American majority neighborhoods and employed Mexican American directors. Thus, NAPP and

Opal Jones both became targets early on for those who believed that Mexican Americans were not fully included in the agency.[19]

The tensions between blacks and Latinos over NAPP reached new heights in September 1966. Early that month, Jones fired Gabriel Yánez, the Latino director of the NAPP field office in Boyle Heights. Jones told Yánez that he was being fired for "failure to give cooperation in the project and to follow the leadership and accept the supervision of the Project Director." She claimed that Yánez had told his aides not to attend meetings called by her and had discouraged residents in his area from involvement in NAPP, because it favored African Americans. Jones also argued that Yánez was contributing to the split between Mexican Americans and African Americans both within NAPP and in Los Angeles at large.[20]

Yánez's firing infuriated many Latinos in Los Angeles; over forty of them picketed NAPP offices and criticized both NAPP and EYOA for showing favoritism toward blacks. Bob Ramirez, a NAPP aide from the Boyle Heights outpost, told a reporter: "until now it was the Negroes who used these tactics. Now we're picketing. And we're going to keep picketing until our problems are recognized."[21]

Jones's initial response to the Mexican American critique was that the outposts had been established after a Welfare Planning Council study of the pockets of poverty in Los Angeles. A few days later, Jones offered to divide the NAPP outposts more equally between black and Latino communities, but this angered black NAPP staff members. In late September Jones penned a memo to Isobel Clark, executive director of the Los Angeles Area Federation of Settlements and Neighborhood Centers, the delegate agency designated to oversee and operate NAPP. In her memo Jones argued that the "*real* issues" were "being obscured in a wave of emotionalism which focuses on the Negro-Mexican-American relationship question and the allocation of War on Poverty funds between the two (2) communities." For Jones, the "real issue" was "management, organization and administration." At the top of her list for firing Yánez was that he "was actively pushing for a widening of schism between the Mexican-American and Negro poverty communities." In addition, she argued that he had failed to heed her instructions and ignored NAPP procedures. Also, she had received a number of complaints against him from NAPP clients and staff. Indeed, as early as June she had written a memo to Yánez scolding him for his "insulting remarks" toward her and his "lack of cooperation." Again, at the end of her letter to Clark, she addressed the issue of racial strife in the War on Poverty and racial favoritism by NAPP. She argued that "despite the fact that there are those who claim that the program discriminates against others in favor of the Negro community, an objective analysis of the facts will prove this is not true."[22]

Despite her protests of nonfavoritism, under extreme pressure and at the insistence of the Federation of Settlements board of directors, Jones rehired Yánez a few days later, but the damage had been done. Irene Tovar, the Latina director of the NAPP outpost in Pacoima, resigned in protest over Yánez's firing, arguing that the incident made "it very clear . . . that I can no longer work within the framework of NAPP." Tovar serves as an example of an activist who served in both cultural empowerment organizations and the War on Poverty. Long active in Mexican American causes, she would be a member of the Chicano Moratorium Committee, which organized in opposition to the Vietnam War in 1970. At the time of her resignation from NAPP, Tovar succinctly summed up the racial tensions and trouble that lay ahead for the War on Poverty in Los Angeles: "What's good for Watts and the civil rights movement is not necessarily good for the Mexican-American community."[23]

The issue of Mexican American representation in NAPP dominated correspondence, meeting minutes, and agendas of NAPP, the Federation of Settlements, and EYOA from late 1966 through 1967. In August 1966, prior to the Jones/Yánez controversy, Luevano wrote Ed Roybal that some Mexican Americans were putting pressure on Isobel Clark of the Federation of Settlements to make NAPP more representative. On October 1 Clark met with Roybal, Representative George Brown, and the directors of NAPP and Teen Post to discuss Mexican American complaints. In the opening line of her Federation of Settlements Executive Director's Report for September-October 1966, Clark wrote, "Crucial issues, relative to ethnic group participation and representation in federally funded programs continue to create problems primarily among the Mexican-American constituents of NAPP, Teen

Post and Head Start projects." The board of directors of the Federation of Settlements discussed NAPP as "having grave problems" related to black/Mexican American relations. At the November board meeting, where the Personnel Committee recommended that Yánez be reinstated, Jones asked for and received a vote of confidence from the board of directors. At the December meeting of the EYOA-NAPP Project Committee, Jones raised concerns about a "major confrontation with the Mexican-American community and the Negro community" about representation within NAPP.[24]

Interracial conflicts continued to fester within NAPP in 1967. In January the minutes of the Federation of Settlements board of directors meeting again reflected the board's overriding concern with the "implementation of the number of Mexican Americans participating in NAPP." The board noted that the Federation of Settlements needed "to offer assistance to [the] Project director in funding and hiring Mexican Americans." The issue raised its head again in May, when Jones fired Mrs. Hernandez, a NAPP aide, for being "bigoted against Negroes." Like Yánez, Hernandez was also later reinstated to her job. Later that month, NAPP leaders met with representatives of the Mexican American United Council of Community Organizations (UCCO) to discuss "NAPP aides imbalance." In June they met again, and NAPP committed itself to hiring more aides. In the NAPP Quarterly Report for April–June 1967, Jones reported that the lack of Mexican Americans in NAPP was "a continual problem" for the agency. She also noted that she had had "many meetings and conferences . . . to involve more Mexican Americans" in NAPP.[25]

Congressman Roybal tried to use the situation to improve Mexican Americans' involvement in the War on Poverty. He wrote a Mexican American NAPP employee that Yánez's "unofficial dismissal . . . was . . . unfortunate. It did, however, bring to the forefront a troublesome problem of long-standing, as well as highlight the many inequities which should have been resolved long ago." Clearly, Roybal was troubled by the ongoing and escalating tensions between blacks and Mexican Americans in Los Angeles and also by the small number of NAPP outposts in Mexican American neighborhoods. He noted that he hoped "to correct" the lack of such outposts "by encouraging more of our organizations to sponsor additional Teen Post programs," also adding that he hoped "through the cooperation of all concerned, the Mexican-American community will eventually receive the attention due them in the anti-poverty war."[26]

Roybal continued his efforts to ensure NAPP representation in Mexican American neighborhoods. In 1967 he and Congressmen Hawkins and Brown, along with Bert Corona, president of the Mexican American Political Association (MAPA), met with Opal Jones to plan the implementation of increased Mexican American representation in NAPP. The following year Roybal and Corona visited Jones at NAPP headquarters, and Jones later wrote Roybal, expressing her appreciation for Roybal's help. She told the congressman, "it was like our old association back at the Avalon Center. . . . I am glad that we were able to be together again after our years of absence." She also thanked Corona, whom she called a "life-saver. . . . He recognizes, as I do, the importance of our teamwork and cooperation together, for that will be the only way that we will make it." Clearly, Jones, Corona, Roybal, and others were trying to make interracialism work. But any attempts and successes at interracial cooperation were limited.[27]

The NAPP divestment/Opal Jones controversy raises some important questions about gender roles in the implementation of the War on Poverty. Did Jones's gender play any role in her being fired? Was her organization targeted by Yorty because she was a woman? No evidence exists to answer either question affirmatively. Indeed, Jones's political association with Hawkins, her involvement in civil rights causes, and the effective community organizing NAPP had accomplished were the most likely reasons for the attacks against her, yet her gender cannot be discounted as a factor. Although Opal Jones rarely spoke openly or directly about women's roles in the War on Poverty and, apparently, did not have any direct links to feminist organizations or theory, her example as a paid director of a War on Poverty program that encouraged participation of the poor challenged OEO's own ideas of women's roles in the War on Poverty. As a woman playing a power game in a traditionally male sphere and in charge of an organization directly connected with empowering women, she was vulnerable to Yorty's attack. In addition, some critics targeted the community-action programs of the War on Poverty as being female-dominated. Jones's position as a prominent woman in the War on Poverty in Los Angeles made her a target. Her experience with NAPP demonstrated the difficulty women of color faced working in male-dominated interracial organizations.

At any rate, NAPP remained active through the early 1970s. By 1968 over two thousand adults had served as NAPP aides; of that number, 78 percent had found employment elsewhere after completing their twelve months with NAPP. Over 50 percent of them had been unemployed prior to joining NAPP. In 1969 OEO revamped NAPP's structure to downplay the community-action focus of the agency. Outposts became neighborhood centers and aides (Jones's change agents) became workers. NAPP focused on providing social and psychological benefits, self-help and mutual aid, improved service delivery, and institutional change for the residents of poor neighborhoods. In 1970 NAPP's five areas of emphasis included Consumer Education and Action, Education, Job Development and New Careers, Social Welfare, and Neighborhood Improvement. By the mid-70s the agency centered its efforts on three programs: Comprehensive Neighborhood Centers, New Careers, and Drug Abuse. It implemented those programs with three approaches—service delivery, community mobilization, and opportunities enhancement.[28]

EYOA Decentralization and Interracial Strife

In addition to divesting EYOA of its control over NAPP, OEO and others wanted to decentralize the agency and bring CAPs closer to the people by creating more agencies. Luevano and Maldonado believed decentralization would be beneficial. As Latinos they were pleased that the plan included a proposed CAP for East Los Angeles. Shriver courted Governor Brown and Congressman Hawkins, people he knew would be in general agreement with the idea. Hawkins initially resisted the idea, because he worried that all unincorporated areas in Los Angeles would want a CAP if East L.A. received one. His disgust with EYOA and Yorty, however, eventually won out, and he agreed to the decentralization plan.[29]

Yorty agreed to the plan at about the same time that Hawkins did. Although in some ways the agreement meant a loss of power for Yorty, he saw the Latino vote as critical to his bid for reelection. By showing support for a community-action program in heavily Latino East Los Angeles, he assured himself some political support there. Yorty agreed to the arrangement on May 2; several days later, the EYOA board accepted the reorganization plan. Shriver sent Yorty a note thanking him for his support of the plan: "I am sure your presence contributed significantly to the outcome. . . . Thank you . . . for your cooperation in bringing about these new arrangements. Your help will be essential to the success of the war against poverty in Los Angeles."[30] At the end of the letter, Shriver included the following handwritten note: "I was particularly pleased that Angelenos themselves were able to work out their differences successfully without intervention from Washington."[31] Based on their prior bickering, Shriver's letter was almost certainly tongue-in-cheek—while Yorty had been more willing to cooperate on this issue than others, he had been the primary stumbling block in the overall EYOA controversy. Furthermore, Los Angeles had not solved this crisis on its own. It would not have been settled but for direct intervention from the Office of Economic Opportunity and Shriver.

At any rate, the agreement had been achieved, and EYOA no longer existed as the only government agency–controlled CAP in Los Angeles County. On August 11, 1966, OEO established new CAAs in Pasadena, Long Beach, Compton-Willowside, and East Los Angeles–Whittier.[32] Some of these new agencies had been created to bring the War on Poverty to Los Angeles's Latino population.

The disparity in poverty assistance was one reason Latino groups pressured OEO to decentralize EYOA in 1966. The Eastland Community Action Council (ECAC), based in East Los Angeles, was one of the four CAAs designated by OEO to replace some of the area covered by EYOA. That organization did not last long. In January 1969 OEO decertified ECAC, because it failed to meet a deadline to conform to federal rules. In truth ECAC had become a battleground for Mexican American groups and was never effective as a community-action agency. In fact many Latino groups (such as the Mexican American Political Association, or MAPA) requested that OEO decertify ECAC due to inefficiencies and its failure to fully include the poor. Some asked EYOA to cover their area again, as long as the agency would let community representatives determine policy. In January 1969 EYOA once again took over operation of OEO programs in East Los Angeles.[33]

The remarriage between Latinos and EYOA did not last long. Latinos consistently protested the hiring practices of EYOA. In 1968 only 37 of EYOA's 260 staff members were Latino, while 106 were white and 100 were black. In 1969 the Mexican American community representatives on the EYOA board demanded more cooperation, information, training, and respect from their colleagues and the EYOA staff. A number of Mexican Americans appeared at the EYOA board meeting in June of that year to protest what they saw as unfair hiring practices by EYOA. Of 260 EYOA employees at that time, only 37 were Mexican American and only 8 of those were professional staff. In October 1971, 50 Latino employees walked out, accusing EYOA of bias. Congressman Roybal sent an angry letter to the EYOA Board of Directors claiming that the "recent walkout of Mexican American workers has raised serious legal and moral issues dealing with racial equity at EYOA." He also wrote OEO acting director Phil Sánchez, warning him that waiting "would be a dangerous mistake, and an act of negligence." He urged Sánchez "to intervene so that racial equity can be obtained and a most serious confrontation between these two groups [blacks and Latinos] prevented." His letters were of little avail—EYOA fired the employees in November. After months of protests, however, they were rehired in April 1972.[34]

Also in 1971, representatives from the Congress of Mexican-American Unity and the Chicano Caucus, reflecting the community-control ideology of the Chicano movement, wrote to OEO demanding direct funding to Chicano organizations that served the poor. They argued that the EYOA had "seriously shortchanged the Chicano poor in its allocation of resources" and that it had a discriminatory, anti-Chicano hiring pattern. The group went on to claim that "without a total rearrangement of the EYOA power relationships, something which would cause great friction and conflict between the Chicano and the Black communities and is therefore not a worthwhile effort, we cannot get equity in funding, in attention, or in treatment." The caucus also sent letters to key members of Congress. Saying that they were "stung by the repeated and continuing insensitivity of . . . EYOA to the special needs of the Mexican-American poor," EYOA delegate agencies had formed the Chicano Caucus in order to seek direct OEO funding.[35]

In the meantime, Congressman Gus Hawkins organized a meeting of black leaders "to consider the best strategy for coping with the many attacks being made by Mexican Americans against agencies by blacks." The idea for the group originated from Hawkins's assistant, Charles Knox, who proposed organizing the group to Hawkins in November 1971. Knox wrote Hawkins that "unless black leaders confront brown leaders with our understanding of what they are doing and its ill effects the problem will mushroom beyond repair. . . . Obviously [Ed Roybal] is having difficulty in rationally handling the pressure by the radical elements in his community." After Hawkins gave his approval, the group, including Opal Jones and Thomas Kilgore, met twice in 1972, with racial strife at EYOA being their primary concern.[36]

When the federal government in August 1972 announced plans to discontinue EYOA, bickering between blacks and Latinos within EYOA intensified. Upon hearing the news of the Nixon administration's plans, Ernest Sprinkles, the African American director of EYOA, called the decision "the plan to eliminate black poverty program directors in this region." His statement incensed Latinos, who accused Sprinkles of being responsible for the split between African American and Latino employees within EYOA.[37]

The reorganization of EYOA in 1972 into the Greater Los Angeles Community Action Agency (GLACAA) did not change the relationship between the organization and its Latino employees. In 1974 the Chicano Coalition, with director Irene Tovar, the former NAPP aide who had resigned in the Gabriel Yánez firing controversy, charged GLACAA with being "as ineffective as was EYOA" in terms of hiring Mexican Americans. At the time, 44 percent of GLACAA employees were black and only 25 percent Mexican American. The Chicano Coalition initiated a lawsuit against GLACAA for its failure to fund projects in Mexican American neighborhoods. The lawsuit, brought by the Chicano Coalition on behalf of Latino employees, alleged that GLACAA was "not only incapable of equitably administering social service programs, as they affect the Chicano community, but also seriously discriminates in its hiring and promotional patterns." In 1975 GLACAA and the Chicano Coalition settled the lawsuit. Under the terms of the agreement, GLACAA was to increase its Latino workforce from 25 percent to 30 percent by June 15, 1975; by 1977, the GLACAA workforce was to consist of 35 percent Latino, 35 percent black, 20 percent Anglo, and 5 percent Asian employees.[38]

Interracial conflicts plagued GLACAA for the remainder of its existence. In December, 1975, the Los Angeles County Board of Supervisors ordered the GLACAA board to solve its ethnic, racial, and financial problems or fire its director, Ralph Fertig. In the meeting, Harry Hufford, the county chief administrative officer, told the Board of Supervisors that GLACAA had "fallen victim to a bureaucratic tug-of-war largely along racial and ethnic lines." Apparently, black employees wanted Fertig out, claiming that he had aligned himself with GLACAA's Latino employees. When the Jimmy Carter administration shut down GLACAA in 1978, it was as much because of unsettled interracial conflict as waste and inefficiency. With the death of GLACAA, the official, government-agency-controlled War on Poverty in Los Angeles ended.[39]

The divisions between the Latino and African American communities in Los Angeles over the EYOA/GLACAA version of the War on Poverty remained unbridgeable. Blacks tended to view the War on Poverty, especially its community-action aspect, as a logical extension of the democratization of American society initiated by the black civil rights movement. Indeed, Opal Jones herself had long been involved in civil rights organizations and had actively supported her friend Tom Bradley's election to the city council in 1963. She provided an important link between the black freedom struggle, government liberalism, and the War on Poverty. In addition, many of the black poor, who had been segregated by whites through discrimination in housing and jobs, attached themselves to the black separatist philosophies of the Nation of Islam and showed an unwillingness to align themselves with any other racial or ethnic group. Latinos comprised the largest minority group in Los Angeles, and many believed they should have an equal share of the War on Poverty services. Their growing population and burgeoning cultural and political activism led some Latinos to demand more programs and services from the local War on Poverty.

Thus, the African American and Latino communities in Los Angeles were pitted against one another along racial lines instead of united together along class lines. This reflected, in part, the shift of the civil rights movement to black power and group-identity politics and the concomitant growth of the Chicano movement. This racial animosity was most clearly expressed in EYOA through NAPP. The only EYOA program that incorporated poor residents, NAPP struggled throughout its existence with racial divisiveness, whether it was over the number and location of NAPP outposts or the number and ethnicity of NAPP aides. NAPP became the chief battleground between African Americans informed by black power and Mexican Americans influenced by the emerging Chicano movement. The political, geographical, and social chasms that separated blacks from Latinos hindered the creation of a sustained protest group to pressure Yorty and local elites to make EYOA more representational and democratic. Ultimately, both groups would look outside EYOA to use the framework of the War on Poverty to advance the cause of the black and Chicano freedom struggles. Indeed, the EYOA/GLACAA failure led to the creation of independent, ethnically nationalist antipoverty agencies in African American and Mexican American neighborhoods in Los Angeles.

Chapter 4
"We're from Watts . . . Mighty, mighty Watts!"
The Watts Labor Community Action Committee and Black Power

DISAPPOINTED WITH THE antipoverty agency agreement engineered by LeRoy Collins and disenchanted with the city-controlled EYOA, some African Americans in Los Angeles looked for alternative avenues for involvement in the War on Poverty. Many questioned why they should participate in a corrupt system controlled by white elites. For some African Americans in Los Angeles, an appealing answer to their dilemma was to create a black community-controlled antipoverty agency. That organization was the Watts Labor Community Action Committee (WLCAC). Created by labor leaders in an attempt to organize the poor in Watts, the WLCAC reflected the shifting emphasis in the black freedom movement from integration to economic self-determination and black power. In addition, the community-action framework of the War on Poverty, which advocated the "maximum feasible participation of the poor" in the formation and operation of antipoverty agencies in their local communities, encouraged the development of WLCAC as an African American community-action agency. As blacks sought to define freedom in ways that focused on economic nationalism and cultural and political empowerment, the WLCAC served as an antipoverty organization with an Afro American focus. Through the "community union" model of the WLCAC, community activists in Watts fought their own War on Poverty, attempting to define African Americans' economic, cultural, and political freedom.

WLCAC and the Unions

After Watts erupted in August 1965, the federal and local governments as well as private organizations began to pay more attention to the Los Angeles area. The recipient of much of this liberal guilt and goodwill was the WLCAC. The predecessor to WLCAC had originated shortly before the implementation of the War on Poverty. In 1964 local members of the United Auto Workers and other unions, researchers at the UCLA Institute for Industrial Relations, and a student group from Jordan High School in Watts joined together over shared concern regarding an Area Redevelopment Agency report. That report showed Watts as a place with significant unemployment and low education levels. The union, academic, and student groups started meeting informally to discuss ways to attack these problems.[1]

Local activists joined with labor union representatives and officially founded WLCAC in the early summer of 1965, in part due to disenchantment with the EYOA stalemate. Angered over the holdup of OEO funds caused by Mayor Yorty's intransigence, WLCAC initially formed to pressure OEO for more community representation in the local War on Poverty. Its founders also hoped that WLCAC might be recognized by OEO as a Community Action Agency for the Watts area. Their intent was to use their union skills and organizational experience to increase community participation, provide services to Watts's residents, and—reflecting a strand of political ideology that coursed throughout black history—build a thriving economic base in the community. Tired of the portrayal of Watts's residents as hopeless and helpless, WLCAC organized with specific programmatic goals such as creating a county hospital for the Watts area, a food and clothes bank, child-care and youth centers, and health centers.[2]

Despite its independence and reliance on local residents, WLCAC always retained and remembered its union roots. In a 1975 interview, then WLCAC director Ted Watkins noted that most of WLCAC's operations were self-sustaining but that union funding and support had always been important to the organization. "We are union oriented. We figured, with the help of our union friends and some people at UCLA . . . maybe we could do for Watts what we were doing for people through our unions—organizing them into action groups."[3]

Major labor unions provided financial assistance and formed an advisory board to WLCAC. The unions represented on the board included the United Auto Workers (UAW), the Amalgamated Clothing Workers of America, Building Service Employees, the International Association of Machinists, the Teamsters, the International Longshoremen and Warehousemen, United Packinghouse Workers, and others. In the first two years of WLCAC's existence, these unions contributed a combined $100,000 to its operations. Finally, WLCAC received research and technical assistance from the UCLA Institute of Industrial Relations, which was closely allied with the UAW.[4]

WLCAC's union support was vital to its creation and survival, and the organization was formed as the first "community union" model of a community-action agency. The United Auto Workers in particular was instrumental in the creation of WLCAC. UAW president Walter Reuther and western regional director Paul Schrade canvased local UAW membership in Watts and helped build a core of support for the new organization. The UAW's involvement in the War on Poverty is not surprising—both Reuther and Schrade had actively supported the black freedom movement. Indeed, the UAW had leased a building to H. H. Brookins's United Civil Rights Committee in Los Angeles for one dollar a year in the early 1960s. They saw the War on Poverty as an "opportunity in which long-standing policies and practices were open to question and change" and believed the way to "create change . . . is by building community organizations."[5]

The UAW had been one of the first organizations within the civil rights coalition to focus its efforts on economic justice. Reuther initially endorsed the War on Poverty, telling President Johnson, "We enlist with you for the duration in the war against poverty and want and pledge our full support and cooperation."[6] While the UAW was not completely satisfied with the War on Poverty because it did not focus on jobs or maldistribution of income, Reuther and the UAW leadership saw the War on Poverty as an "opportunity in which long-standing policies and practices were open to question and change."[7]

In March of 1964, after learning that the administration was planning an antipoverty program, Reuther created the Citizens' Crusade against Poverty (CCAP). The CCAP, formed to act as a liaison between the OEO and the poor, was a coalition of labor leaders, civil rights leaders, and individuals on the political left (eventually including Martin Luther King, Jr., A. Philip Randolph, Michael Harrington, Richard Cloward, and Paul Potter of Students for a Democratic Society). In 1965 CCAP established four regional educational training centers (in Chicago, New York, Mississippi, and Delano, California) "to train poor community activists in the intricacies of the poverty program." UAW considered WLCAC a parallel program to the training centers, although WLCAC was the only one of the centers that gave the poor a direct voice in policymaking from the beginning.[8] The UAW saw the War on Poverty as an opportunity to expand the democratic goals of the civil rights movement and moved quickly to support the War on Poverty, especially its stated purpose of community action and organization.

Reuther's support for the federal government's War on Poverty did not endure. Upset over what he saw as a gradual shift from the initial goal of community action and angered over the administration's refusal to expand the domestic budget because of America's involvement with Vietnam, Reuther, especially through CCAP, began to attack the administration. After one harsh CCAP critique of the administration's refusal to expand OEO's budget, Johnson told Califano to tell Reuther and the CCAP board "to cut this stuff out." The CCAP then focused its energies on funding its own community-action programs. In addition to its vital role in creating WLCAC, the UAW initiated a similar program in East Los Angeles, The East Los Angeles Community Union (TELACU), which became the "most influential Chicano organization" in Los Angeles.[9]

In his testimony to the Kerner Commission, Schrade argued that the way to "create change in this nation is by building community organizations." Importantly, Schrade told the commission that these organizations, such as WLCAC, needed to be independent of the trade-union movement and to "determine their own course of action, their own programs." Schrade believed that the UAW had helped the WLCAC build an organization that was both "responsive to the needs of the people, and under the control of the people who live in the community."[10]

The importance of local control was central to the WLCAC. Shortly after its creation, the organization's original chair, Otis T. Ireland, outlined the general philosophy of WLCAC—to involve local residents more completely in the War on Poverty specifically, and in the decisions that affected their lives generally. According to Ireland, the committee would "stress very specific projects in which local residents have expressed an interest, with our members and consultants going door to door in Watts getting the opinions of the residents. We are already making this kind of personal contact, and will continue to make this the major part of our program."[11] A UAW report noted that WLCAC emphasized community participation from "the bottom up, and the inside out, rather than from the top down and the outside in."[12] The concepts of local control, self-empowerment, and self-determination, which would remain central to the philosophy of WLCAC, and merged well with the cultural and economic nationalism of the black power movement.

WLCAC and Ted Watkins

Initially ignored by OEO, WLCAC was "discovered" by the antipoverty agency after the violence in Watts. That discovery was no accident. Shortly after the Watts revolt, WLCAC began a more assertive and persistent effort to urge OEO and the local governments toward antipoverty and direct-action programs. Combined with the placement of Ted Watkins as full-time project administrator for WLCAC in July 1966, WLCAC's new approach led to more generous responses from both local and federal agencies.[13]

Watkins was born in Meridian, Mississippi, in 1912 and moved to the Los Angeles area with his family, as did many other black families from Mississippi and Louisiana, at the onset of the Great Depression in the late 1920s and early 1930s. After high school, Watkins began working for Ford Motor Company and joined the local chapter of the UAW. He gradually rose through the union ranks and eventually became the international representative for UAW.[14]

Watkins's activism went beyond his union activities. In the 1950s and early 1960s, he and his wife, Bernice, involved themselves in various civil rights organizations, including the Watts chapter of the NAACP and the United Civil Rights Committee, to protest poor housing conditions and the lack of services in inner-city Los Angeles. When, in 1966, UAW leadership sought someone with organizational and activist experience who also lived in Watts to serve as WLCAC administrator, Watkins was the logical choice. He provided an important link between civil rights, labor organizing, and community activism. His desire, experience, hard work, and organizing abilities drove WLCAC for almost thirty years.[15]

Watkins's energy and tireless efforts quickly paid dividends, as the WLCAC and its programs began to garner national attention. Indeed, WLCAC became heralded as a national model for community-action agencies. In May 1967 Watkins convinced Robert Kennedy, Joe Clark, and George Murphy, members of the Senate Subcommittee on Manpower, Employment, and Poverty, to visit Watts and WLCAC. The senators left Los Angeles impressed with the WLCAC organization. As a result, in 1967 OEO granted WLCAC over $250,000 for various programs, including consumer services and the operation of a credit union. A credit union was vital to the community, because previously residents had had to go out of the area to obtain a loan. Often they faced problems receiving loan approval because of their race, or they were charged higher interest rates because of where they lived. When he announced the grant, Theodore Berry, director of community-action programs for OEO, described WLCAC as "sound" and "well-organized" and noted that WLCAC already had a "demonstrated record of successful performance."[16]

Other agencies, both public and private, also noticed WLCAC's impressive record and were willing to provide the organization with funding for various programs. That trend continued throughout the 1960s and 1970s. In 1971 WLCAC constructed thirty homes with funds from the state of California and later received an additional $2 million loan from its friends at UAW-Chrysler to purchase property in order to build more residential housing. At about the same time, WLCAC received another of its many grants from the Ford Foundation to pay administrators and project staff and also to establish a Minority Enterprise Small Business Investment Corporation to introduce new commercial ventures to Watts.[17]

WLCAC's focus shifted somewhat in the early 1970s to housing development and commercial ventures, because OEO had designated it a Community Development Corporation (CDC). Congress, led by

Senator Robert Kennedy, passed amendments to the Economic Opportunity Act in 1966 that eventually led to additional amendments in the 1970s allowing for the creation of CDCs. The WLCAC was one of eight CDCs funded, in part, by the Ford Foundation. The idea for CDCs emerged from the Ford Foundation's Gray Areas programs of the early 1960s and the community-action agencies of the War on Poverty. A CDC was "a locally controlled, tax-exempt corporation that operates programs aimed at both immediate relief of severe social and economic disadvantage and at eventual regeneration of its community." The CDC approach targeted low-income areas through a comprehensive approach that emphasized private enterprise and coordination of business, government, and neighborhood efforts. They were designed to be hybrid organizations, "quasi-private and quasi-public." The CDC strategy emphasized community control and planned economic development to address the problems of poverty and unemployment. Its goals included removing community dependence on external forces and providing "individuals with the means necessary for a more fuller [*sic*] participation and integration in society by broadening the distribution of capital, income and opportunities within the community." Thus, CDCs essentially have functioned as publicly funded venture-capital companies that financed the high-risk startup costs of new businesses where the risk was too great to appeal to private capital. That comprehensive and coordinated CDC philosophy guided WLCAC's programs.[18]

WLCAC included some of the War on Poverty programs (such as the Neighborhood Youth Corps) in its repertoire, but most of its programs were its own creations and emphasized community control. In addition to the credit union, they included community ownership and the operation of two service stations, a poultry farm, a grocery store, a truck farm, a coin laundry, a furniture and appliance shop, food-stamp centers, community centers, a commercial center, and a building and supply store. Clearly influenced by the CDC approach, Watkins and the WLCAC used the framework of the War on Poverty in an attempt to build a black economic base in Watts.[19]

Like the national War on Poverty and the EYOA in Los Angeles, the WLCAC, in addition to its community economic programs, focused many of its programs on youth. WLCAC received a number of grants for job training, most of them for disadvantaged youth and school drop-outs. In the summer of 1966, WLCAC received over $300,000 from the Department of Labor for summer recreational and educational facilities for Watts's youth. In fact, by the time of the OEO grant in 1967, WLCAC had already received grants from the Neighborhood Youth Corps (NYC) and from the EYOA for youth employment projects.[20]

As part of that youth emphasis, WLCAC also established the Urban Residential Educational Center in the countrylike setting of Saugus, located in the desert in the extreme northeastern corner of Los Angeles County. There, young people ages sixteen to twenty-four were given vocational education in business, auto repair, and horticulture. They lived at the camp five days a week, returning home on weekends, for one year. The positive influence of WLCAC and its youth programs made noise all the way to the White House. In a 1967 memo to President Johnson, advisor Bill Graham described WLCAC as "successful" in providing training and recreational opportunities for youth.[21]

WLCAC's most significant non-youth-based project was the creation of the Martin Luther King, Jr. Medical Center in South Central Los Angeles. The need for a county hospital facility in the Watts area was one of the primary reasons WLCAC formed in 1964. At that time Watts residents had to travel fifteen miles, often in heavy traffic, to reach a hospital. From WLCAC's inception, the organization and others prodded county, state, and federal officials for a hospital. In 1967 the state and county approved tentative plans for the Watts-Willowbrook hospital and placed Watkins on the commission to oversee the financial plans for the facility. Watkins saw the new hospital not only as filling a health-care need, but also as an economic base for the community. He was right. Since the Martin Luther King, Jr. Hospital opened its doors (the name was changed before the hospital opened in 1971 to honor the slain civil rights leader), more Watts residents have worked there than for any other private or public employer in the area.[22]

To ensure that hospital employees would have somewhere nearby and affordable to live, in the late 1970s WLCAC began construction on a housing project across from the hospital. The project, which included single-family homes along with some apartments, resulted in the construction of over six hundred residences, demonstrating WLCAC's mission as a CDC and its recognition of the hospital as central to the area's economy.[23]

WLCAC also initiated some programs that veered from the normal CAP programs and in some ways resembled old New Deal CCC and WPA projects. In addition to economic programs, WLCAC emphasized improving the quality of life for Watts residents. Irwin Unger has argued that the primary success of the Great Society programs was the improvement of quality of life for the middle class.[24] Watkins and WLCAC knew quality of life was important not only to the middle class, but also to the working class and unemployed in Watts. A WLCAC brochure noted that when it was formed, its "most ambitious purpose was to beautify Watts, to transform the community into a place where anyone of any background or life style would want to live, and to kindle the fire of pride and self respect in its people. WLCAC . . . [believes] that economic power is the first step on the long road to community stability and personal opportunity."[25] Even in materials promoting beautification and quality of life, the WLCAC reflected the black freedom movement's renewed emphasis on economic empowerment.

But, quality of life, undoubtedly, was important to Watkins and the WLCAC. While Lady Bird Johnson was attempting to beautify the country, the WLCAC created eleven small parks, known as vest-pocket parks, on former vacant lots in South Central Los Angeles. The parks included senior-citizen centers, playgrounds, and neighborhood centers on their grounds. WLCAC also helped beautify South Central by planting over twenty-two thousand trees along its streets and in its parks.[26]

The people visiting those parks were overwhelmingly African American, yet a small number of Mexican Americans (roughly 5 percent of the total Watts population of just fewer than thirty thousand in 1965) resided in Watts. With an organization formed under the influence of the black power ethos, an interracial movement of the poor was not necessarily a priority. Indeed, the organization's 1967 report acknowledged that "few channels of communication between [blacks and Mexican Americans] have been opened." WLCAC leadership nevertheless did attempt to address this in a few different ways, through efforts to recruit Mexican American supervisors and enroll Mexican

Americans in WLCAC programs; a field trip to Delano, California, to join Mexican American farmworker children in a Christmas celebration; cultural-heritage training in African American and Mexican American history; and courses in conversational Spanish "as a beginning in encouraging more meaningful communication and acceptance among Negro and Mexican-American youths."[27] Most of those efforts at interracial cooperation, though, were not long-term and did not play a central part in WLCAC's ideology or strategy.

WLCAC and Black Power

Instead, the ideology of black power—particularly the elements of self-definition, community control, and cultural nationalism—infused virtually all WLCAC programs. One of WLCAC's original creations was the New Deal–like Community Conservation Corps (CCC). A brainchild of Watkins, who remembered the New Deal fondly, the CCC was created by combining Neighborhood Youth Corps funding for sixteen- to twenty-one-year-olds and Manpower Development and Training Act (MDTA) demonstration funds for fourteen- to fifteen-year-olds to convert vacant lots into visible playgrounds. The fourteen- to twenty-one-year-olds also supervised a cadet corps of seven- to fifteen-year-olds in group recreation and cultural activities. Begun in the summer of 1966 as a way to keep youth busy in constructive ways, the program combined work-training projects and artistic pursuits. In 1967 alone, over six hundred CCC members made bookshelves for Head Start sites, cleaned streets, help create parks, and learned shop and automotive skills. In addition, they had educational classes, learned about black heritage and culture, and made important material contributions to their community.[28]

WLCAC's CCC differed from the New Deal version in at least one important aspect—the WLCAC program directly reflected the black power movement. Corps members marched through the streets of Watts chanting:

> *We're from Watts, you know,*
> Mighty, mighty Watts!
> *Get outta the way*

Ted Watkins stands outside the WLCAC offices with young applicants for the Watts Community Conservation Corps, July 1, 1967. Courtesy Los Angeles Public Library.

> *Cause here we come.*
> *Soul brothers,*
> *Soul sisters,*
> *Soul city,*
> *Soul town,*
> *Soul world,*
> *Soul people,*
> *Soul now!*[29]

The CCC chant perfectly embodied the symbiotic relationship between the War on Poverty, the WLCAC, and black power. "We're from Watts, you know, / *Mighty, mighty Watts!*" exuded community and cultural pride. "Get outta the way / Cause here we come" demonstrated the personal and community empowerment the CCC and black power brought these teenagers in Watts. It also suggested an impatience and

This float in the Watts Summer Festival Parade in 1968 pays tribute to some of the fallen heroes of the black freedom struggle. The Watts Writers Workshop was one of the WLCAC–sponsored programs that focused on black cultural nationalism. Courtesy Los Angeles Public Library.

immediacy to their cause. And the remaining lines of the chant echoed the celebration of Afro American culture in the 1960s. In their "We're from Watts" call, the teenagers of the CCC merged the causes of the War on Poverty and the evolving black freedom movement.

Central to the philosophy of WLCAC and to its connection to the ideas of black nationalism were the programs that focused on cultural enrichment and black pride. For example, WLCAC encouraged a WPA-like writers' workshop, which turned out film writers, poets, and teachers. Rhodes Scholar Stanley Sanders returned home to Watts and found that "writers, poets, artists flourished. . . . I have not seen during eight years of college life as many personal journals kept and sketches written than in Watts since the 1965 riots." Started in Westminster by screenwriter Budd Schulberg, the workshop, with monetary support from WLCAC, moved to the new Watts Happening Coffeehouse on

103rd in Watts. The WLCAC and other community organizations eventually created the Frederick Douglass House, where writers lived and worked. The workshop disbanded in 1970 as a result of an FBI investigation and a fire that destroyed much of the building. In its short-lived existence, the workshop had helped change the perception of Watts "from the National-Guard-studded streets to an active arena of spiritual and cultural struggle." In addition, the Watts Happening Coffeehouse was constructed by WLCAC as a center for cultural enrichment and intellectual development. Events at Watts Happening included jazz concerts, folk and gospel sing-alongs, artist exhibits, and presentations of plays and poetry.[30]

Perhaps the most explicit example of black pride and the focus on Afro American culture was the Watts Summer Festival.[31] Initiated by a coalition of antipoverty organizations and black nationalist groups, the festival focused on black culture. Founders of the festival included groups such as the WLCAC and Westminster Neighborhood Association and individuals such as Stan Sanders, Booker Griffin—a local radio personality and columnist for the *Los Angeles Sentinel,* Tommy Jacquette—founder of SLANT (Self-Leadership for All Nationalities Today), and Maulana Ron Karenga—founder of the US Organization. The festival was part of an explosion of black nationalist and self-help organizations that occurred in Watts in the years after the violence in 1965. Although the groups may have had differing styles and philosophies—some were cultural nationalists, some emphasized economic nationalism, and others focused on political power—they all supported the ideals of community empowerment and self-definition. New organizations such as SLANT, the Afro-American Cultural Association, the Sons of Watts Improvement Association, Community Pride, Inc., and the Black Man's Self-Image Development Institute appeared, flourished, and actively participated in the festival in the late 1960s. The festival also featured informational booths highlighting the services of various public and private agencies, such as EYOA, the Westminster Neighborhood Association, WLCAC, and NAPP. The festival activities centered on celebrating black culture. Acts such as US Organization boot dancers, Zulu dancers, and trumpeter Hugh Masekela and arts-and-craft booths demonstrating and selling African jewelry and clothing entertained largely black audiences of anywhere from thirty to over one hundred thousand people.[32]

The festival parade highlighted the community celebration. The sponsors of the parade, which included the WLCAC, chose Sargent Shriver to serve as grand marshal of the first parade in August 1966, because he had "done more for urban minorities than any other man in this country."[33] The sponsors may have exaggerated Shriver's contributions, but they understood the importance of the War on Poverty to their community. Its framework had allowed African Americans in Watts to create a community-action agency that had given them some control over economic and cultural issues in their lives. OEO and the War on Poverty had made democracy a little more relevant to the citizens of Watts, who used this expanded democracy to make changes in their community.

It was the confluence of the black power movement with the War on Poverty that enabled these changes to take place. Many in the black freedom struggle in Los Angeles lost their faith in the inclusive philosophy of the integrationist civil rights movement, due to the city's intransigence in the battle over EYOA. The black power movement's emphasis on economic and cultural nationalism merged with the War on Poverty's focus on community participation in the form of the WLCAC. The Watts Summer Festival Parade was one example of the celebration of cultural power made possible by the War on Poverty and the black power movement.

Not all advocates of black power approved of the festival, however. Marxists and political nationalist groups such as the Black Panther Party and the Black United Front opposed the festival's focus on cultural nationalism, referring to the celebration as a "darky carnival." Elaine Brown, the minister of information of the LA chapter of the Black Panther Party, denounced the festival as a "darky parade," referred to Tommy Jacquette a "bootlicker," and called festival supporters "lackeys" of the power structure. The Panthers saw the festival as "a counter-revolutionary strategy to pacify blacks and to suppress the protest impulses throbbing in the black community." The verbal attacks on the festival by the Panthers and others demonstrate the varieties of black nationalism that flourished in the late 1960s and early 1970s.

Sargent Shriver, director of the Office of Economic Opportunity, awards a trophy to Tamu Harper, winner of the Miss Watts Beauty Contest in 1966. The contest, part of the Watts Summer Festival, reflected the festival's connection to the cultural ethos of the black power movement, and Shriver's presence demonstrated the connection of the War on Poverty to black cultural empowerment in Watts. Courtesy Los Angeles Public Library.

Crowds line Central Avenue for the second Watts Summer Festival Parade, August 14, 1967. Courtesy Los Angeles Public Library.

Many groups called themselves black nationalists, but their strategies and approaches differed greatly. Cultural nationalists, Marxists, economic nationalists, and political revolutionaries all might have agreed on the need for black power, but they did not all agree on what that meant or how to achieve it.[34]

Despite these divisions within the black power movement, the Watts Summer Festival and Parade flourished through the late 1960s and early 1970s; indeed, over one hundred thousand celebrated the festivals in 1972 and 1973. The festivals remained focused on black culture and pride. The 1967 Summer Festival program featured a photo of grand marshal Muhammad Ali with the title, "Pride and Progress." The 1973 festival featured Jesse Jackson giving his "I Am Somebody" speech, dressed in an African dashiki. Festival attendance then

The WLCAC float in the Watts Summer Festival Parade, August 14, 1967.
Courtesy Los Angeles Public Library.

declined in the years following, and the festival disappeared altogether
for a few years, before reappearing for good in 1979. Despite ups and
downs in attendance and participation, the Watts Summer Festival and
Parade had connected the War on Poverty and black nationalism, and it
had helped restore a sense of community and cultural pride to the
residents of Watts. The festival sponsors had hoped "it would channel
black anger and discontent into meaningful black pride as well as provide jobs and entrepreneurial opportunities and experience for many
blacks." The festival had certainly succeeded in creating black pride,
and WLCAC had played a large part in the festival and its significance.[35]

WLCAC also used direct action to improve the lives of the residents of Watts. From picketing a tire dump for removal from their
community, to badgering Douglas Aircraft to hire Watts residents to
work at their new plant, to taking over the Watts Towers and making it

a more attractive community emblem, to demonstrating against the county Bureau of Public Assistance, WLCAC led the people of Watts in community-action demonstrations. WLCAC programs such as the CCC actively involved the youth of Watts in the betterment of their community. Neighborhood centers created a space where residents could come together to discuss and debate issues, as well as organize for concrete gains in their community. The residents of the area were thus able to gain some control over their own community and their own lives.[36]

WLCAC's success at creating an innovative community agency controlled by local residents did not go unnoticed. Some of the praise came from an obvious corner. Paul Schrade, of the UAW, called the WLCAC "one of the most effective programs in the United States." Bill Jones, the director of the Los Angeles Model Cities Program, also had high praise for the WLCAC. Noting that the organization worked primarily with unskilled people, many of them school dropouts with criminal records, Jones argued that the WLCAC did a much better job in training "hard-to-reach kids" than the public schools.[37] The Los Angeles City Council also honored WLCAC. While the city's own community-action agency was embroiled in politics and controversy, WLCAC showed that the War on Poverty could work. In a 1968 resolution, the city council praised WLCAC for developing an organization that "while improving the community provides work for the unemployed youth of the community, offers the learning of invaluable skills and instills a true sense of pride in their neighborhood."[38]

Watkins himself received much praise. A Ford Foundation administrator in 1975 thought of Watkins as "a great man." He described Watkins as "an organizer, a person who thinks up more ideas in a day than most of us do in a month, and then [he] puts them into operation." Watkins was both a thinker and a doer, dominating the WLCAC for over thirty years. Most of the organization's programs were his ideas, and he made sure they operated smoothly. Ted Watkins was the face, heart, and soul of the WLCAC.[39]

Indeed, out of the evolution of the black freedom movement, the War on Poverty, and the Watts uprising, Watkins and others created an agency whose ideology reflected its intellectual origins and social mi-

lieu. Born of the black freedom struggle, WLCAC expanded the democratic goals of the civil rights movement. Emerging at the time of a
renewed interest in black culture and heritage, WLCAC programs
brought black pride and black power to the residents of Watts. Inspired
by the War on Poverty, the organization opened the doors of economic
opportunity for African Americans and encouraged community action.
Reflecting disenchantment with the white establishment in Los Angeles in the period of the Watts uprising, WLCAC focused on community control and development of its own programs.

The WLCAC remains an active and vital community-action agency
today, although maintaining its community-action focus has become
more difficult as the community changes. Much of the credit for its
survival is due to Watkins, the heart and soul of the committee. When he
died in November 1993, Ted Watkins was eulogized by the *Los Angeles
Times* as a "master at coaxing money out of the federal government."[40] He
was more than that—he had organized an agency that gave the black
residents of Watts some sense of control over their community. Indeed,
Mayor Tom Bradley lauded Watkins at his memorial for having organized
"the best community action program in the nation."[41]

Watkins was also significant because he served as an important link
between various movements of the 1960s and 1970s—the black freedom
struggle, the labor movement, and the War on Poverty. Clearly, he saw
the War on Poverty as an extension of the civil rights and labor movements' efforts to democratize America. His leadership of WLCAC provides further evidence that War on Poverty community organizations
need to be seen as part of the "long civil rights movement."

Yet WLCAC survived and flourished due to more factors than Ted
Watkins. It flourished because it was in reality what the War on Poverty
had intended: a legitimate *community* action agency. Its founders were
all middle-class and working-class union members who lived in the
community, and it allowed all residents, no matter what their income
level, to participate in community decisions and receive services. It
worked *with* the people of the community as well as *for* them. It created programs to target the specific needs of that area, and it has always
been controlled by people in that community, not by bureaucratic experts or local politicians. Perhaps most importantly, it flourished be-

cause it resonated with African Americans' desire for economic and cultural empowerment.

Over the years, WLCAC remained viable because it remained a largely black organization. Thwarted by the institutional racism of city politics in Los Angeles and disappointed by the failure or attempted interracial alliances, blacks turned to WLCAC as the black freedom movement shifted from integration to economic self-determination and black power. As a black antipoverty organization, WLCAC provided more of a sense of community control for its residents than EYOA ever did.

Despite its successes, WLCAC has not ended poverty in the Watts area—far from it. Indeed, the unemployment rate in Watts still hovers around 20 percent. Much of that unemployment is the result of the loss of low-skilled factory jobs to automation and the movement of jobs to the suburbs. In addition, local branches of state offices overseeing fair employment and housing have closed down due to budget cuts. Finally, changes in the global marketplace—the shift from manufacturing to service-industry jobs, moving factories to other countries for lower labor costs, and corporations' growing preference for temporary employment—have further damaged the inner-city poor in America. Forces beyond WLCAC's control have prevented it from making a major economic impact on the poor of Los Angeles.[42]

The circumstances behind WLCAC's own creation, though, have also prevented it from becoming a dominant influence in the lives of the poor of Los Angeles. Brought into being in part as a response to EYOA's failure to include true community representation, formed at the time of the Watts revolt and the growth of black nationalism and the black power movement, WLCAC was a predominantly black organization, representing what was then an overwhelmingly African American area of Los Angeles. As such, it has not had to worry much about interference from the local governments or the white establishment. On the other hand, because of its location in one minority neighborhood, it has never made a significant impact outside of that area. With its focus on economic and cultural self-determination, WLCAC has not created an interracial coalition with low-income groups of other races, such as Latinos or the growing number of Asian poor.

Driving down one of the main streets of Watts today—Slauson or Central Avenue—it becomes evident that Watts has changed. Many of the signs above the stores and businesses are now exclusively in Spanish. The black population in South Central Los Angeles decreased 17 percent in the 1980s, while the Latino population burgeoned. In 1980, 90 percent of the population of Watts was black; by 1990, Watts was 50 percent black and 50 percent Latino. As early as 1980, 40 percent of the homes in Watts were being purchased by Latinos. In that same year, for the first time, more Latino children than black children were born at Martin Luther King, Jr. Hospital. By 2000, Latinos constituted well over 50 percent of the population of Watts. Programs focusing on black cultural empowerment did not resonate as strongly with some of the newer residents of Watts. As a result, WLCAC began to reincorporate programs celebrating Latino culture similar to those it had attempted in the 1960s.[43]

The War on Poverty led to the WLCAC, which arose out of the black freedom movement and African American efforts to achieve self-determination, cultural identity, and empowerment. And the WLCAC became a powerful symbol for its community. Through its service and jobs programs, but particularly through its focus on cultural empowerment, the WLCAC connected the residents of Watts to the War on Poverty, their Afro American heritage and culture, and "Mighty, mighty Watts" itself.

The WLCAC shows that the "long war on poverty" has continued well beyond the 1960s and 1970s. It also demonstrates one way in which the shifting boundaries of race shaped the development of the War on Poverty in Los Angeles and the War on Poverty helped mold and alter those racial and cultural boundaries. But those boundaries in Los Angeles were also influenced by War on Poverty organizations in Latino neighborhoods—and the WLCAC was not the only community-union model War on Poverty agency in Los Angeles.

Chapter 5
The East Los Angeles Community Union
The Chicano Movement and
the Community Union Model

AFRICAN AMERICANS CREATED the WLCAC about the same time that Mexican Americans in Los Angeles, in part due to their competition with blacks for War on Poverty funds, sought to create their own institutions focused on cultural self-determination in East Los Angeles, a predominantly Mexican American community about ten miles northeast of Watts and just east of downtown. The population of that community was growing exponentially. Indeed, the number of persons of Mexican descent living in Los Angeles doubled from over 150,000 in 1950 to just fewer than 300,000 in 1960. During the postwar period, Mexican Americans, who had lived in scattered communities throughout greater Los Angeles, became increasingly segregated into East Los Angeles.[1]

Bordered on the west and north by the city of Los Angeles, on the northeast by Monterey Park, on the southwest by Montebello, and to the south by the city of Commerce, greater East Los Angeles constitutes eight square miles and is composed of at least five historically distinct communities: Highland Park, Lincoln Heights, Boyle Heights, El Sereno, and Unincorporated East Los Angeles. Highland Park, the furthest northwest of the East L.A. communities, is also the most economically successful, with lower rates of unemployment and poverty than the other communities. Lincoln Heights, just south of Highland Park, had a significant Italian American population until the post–World War II period, when Mexican Americans began arriving in significant numbers. Boyle Heights, just south of Lincoln Heights, maintained large Jewish and Japanese American populations until after World War II, when Jews began migrating to the Fairfax district of Los Angeles and Japanese Americans moved elsewhere after losing their homes during the war. It was during the 1940s and 1950s that Mexican Americans began moving into residential areas in Boyle Heights. El Sereno, just north of the unincorporated area of East Los Angeles, contains the campus of California State University, Los Angeles. The Unincorporated East Los Angeles was originally known as Belvedere and contained a mixture of Anglo, Russian, and Jewish residents. Mexican American residents, who began to move into the area in significant numbers in the 1920s, called the central area of the community "La Maravilla."[2]

In 1965 over three-quarters of East LA residents were Latino and 30 percent were Spanish speakers. East Los Angeles had become the major entry point for immigrants from Mexico and Latin America. About one-half of residents had been born in the United States; 47 percent had been born in Mexico and the other 3 percent in other Latin American nations. Unemployment stood at double the county average, and one-quarter of the area's residents lived below the poverty level. The average East L.A. worker's real income in 1976 was lower than it had been in 1970. East L.A. suffered both from problems of the central city—industrial decline, poverty, and crime, as well as those of an older suburban community—high cost of land and business-center decay. Indeed, 80 percent of East L.A. residents worked in blue-collar jobs that were gradually disappearing. Over 75 percent worked outside the community, a sign of the limited capital in East L.A.[3]

The War on Poverty and Interracial Conflict

Within the system of white segregation and racism in Los Angeles, blacks and Latinos had a history of disagreement and strife as a result of competition for jobs that began during World War II and continued into the 1960s. Several attempts at interracial coalitions were made during and after the war, including the Southeast Interracial Council, the Council for Civic Unity, and the County Committee for Interracial Progress, but they all floundered on the rocks of anticommunism and divisions between and within black and Mexican American communities. A small group of black activists formed the Democratic Minority Conference in the early 1960s and attempted to create an alliance between the city's blacks and Chicanos, but did not succeed. When

Mexican American city councilman Ed Roybal, who had served on the council since 1949, left after his election to Congress in 1962, he was replaced by Gilbert Lindsay, an African American. The replacement of the only Mexican American council member with an African American angered some in the Latino community. When the United Civil Rights Committee (UCRC) formed in 1963, it refused to include Mexican Americans as members. As a result, Congressman Roybal and newspaper publisher Leon Washington arranged a meeting of Mexican American and black leaders at the County Hall of Administration in November 1963. According to John Buggs, executive director of the Los Angeles County Commission on Human Relations, the meeting "grew out of a conviction on the part of Messers. Roybal and Washington that now is the time for these two minority groups to cooperate; that it would be tragic if tension and conflict were to develop between them." Buggs, Roybal, and Washington's worst fears were realized when the meeting resulted without agreement or coalition. In May 1965, just a few months prior to the violence in Watts, the County Human Relations Commission reported a high degree of tension between blacks and Latinos. Indeed, a 1965 study found that only 16 percent of Mexican Americans surveyed supported any type of black-Chicano coalition.[4]

Mexican American leaders responded to Watts and the creation of the War on Poverty in Los Angeles with a determination to compete with African Americans for War on Poverty programs and funds. This competition occurred at a time when traditional integrationist Mexican American leadership organizations—such as the League of United Latin American Citizens (LULAC), the GI Forum, and the Mexican American Political Association (MAPA)—were being challenged by younger people who in the late 1960s, inspired by black nationalism, would form the separatist, economic-nationalist Brown Berets and La Raza Unida. Traditional Mexican American organizations hesitated to align with African Americans, because they wanted to ensure that Mexican Americans received their share of the War on Poverty pie. Younger leaders opposed aligning with African American civil rights organizations, because of a separatist ethnic and economic ideology. Both hoped to use the War on Poverty to create organizations and programs benefiting Mexican American communities. Thus, the War on Poverty, as Rodolpho Acuña has argued, encouraged competition between African Americans and Latinos, "each wanting control of their portion of the windfall funds that suddenly came to the communities."[5]

Mexican American leaders' disenchantment with the War on Poverty in Los Angeles began at the time of the consolidation of EYOA, which some Mexican Americans saw as being created to appease blacks after the Watts revolt. When the YOB held informational meetings about the formation of EYOA in East Los Angeles, few people attended. The creation of EYOA failed to generate any enthusiasm among Mexican Americans in Los Angeles.[6]

Shortly after the EYOA settlement arranged by LeRoy Collins, LULAC president Alfred Hernandez argued that perhaps Mexican Americans "should resort to marches, sit-ins, and demonstrations." In October 1965 Congressman Ed Roybal, who represented East Los Angeles, told OEO that his constituents felt they were not getting "a square deal" from OEO and that the Johnson administration had a policy of "Negroes first." He observed that perhaps Mexican Americans would "have to riot to get attention." Roybal also predicted racial strife in Los Angeles within a year "unless something is done to indicate that the Mexican-American group is getting a good deal." The message was not lost on OEO director Sargent Shriver. On the memo informing him of Roybal's complaints, Shriver wrote, "We *should* be doing much more with Mexican-Americans."[7]

Latino groups began to organize to combat the fact that blacks were receiving more War on Poverty funds than were Mexican Americans. These efforts were, for the most part, focused on inclusion and representation. Rudy Ramos, the GI Forum lead attorney, complained to the White House that the predominantly Mexican American community of East Los Angeles had lower incomes than the Watts area, yet it had received little War on Poverty funding. In September a group of Latinos wired Shriver urging him to investigate the distribution of programs in Los Angeles. The writers of the telegram, who included representatives of MAPA, LULAC, the GI Forum, and the Community Service Organization, noted that the principal purpose of such an investigation would be "to instill in the Mexican-American community the

belief that the Office of Economic Opportunity is really interested in
their plight and will correct those inequities." Another purpose of an
investigation would be "to bring a halt to the rising bitter feelings of the
Mexican-American in the streets that antipoverty funds and job opportunities are going principally to Negroes."[8]

Mexican American political activism in relation to the War on
Poverty during this period shifted from inclusion and representation to
self-determination and community control. In 1966, at the time of the
NAPP Opal Jones/Gabriel Yánez controversy, a group of young Mexican Americans led by Vickie Castro, inspired by the War on Poverty's
community-action ideal, created the Young Citizens for Community
Action (soon to become the Young Chicanos for Community Action, or
YCCA). These young people's experience in neighborhood and community improvement increased their awareness of and pride in their
ethnic identity, and they began to create events focusing on Chicano
culture, history, and politics. Led by David Sánchez, the group became
the Brown Berets in 1968, emphasizing their shift to issues of group
empowerment and cultural nationalism.[9]

Other evidence of the influence of the burgeoning Chicano movement included the establishment of an activist Mexican American Legal Defense and Education Fund (MALDEF) office in Los Angeles. In
addition, Latino students at various colleges and universities in Southern California formed student organizations such as the United Mexican American Students (UMAS), which organized and politicized
young Latinos and led to student strikes, or "blowouts," at several high
schools in East Los Angeles in 1968. These walkouts were the first
significant events of the Chicano movement in East Los Angeles. Two
years later and five years after Watts, in August 1970, Latino anti–
Vietnam War demonstrators and police clashed in Los Angeles in "the
largest protest demonstration ever mounted by people of Mexican descent living in the United States." Chicano activists organized the protest because of the inordinate number of Chicanos being killed in the
war. As part of this clash, police killed three Mexican Americans, including Rubén Salazar, a reporter for the *Los Angeles Times*. The incident, combined with already growing student and community activism,

led to increased pressure for self-determination and community control by Chicanos in the War on Poverty in Los Angeles.[10]

A Chicano War on Poverty

As the Chicano movement coincided with and informed Mexican American efforts for self-determination through the framework and programs of the War on Poverty, Mexican Americans began to use the War on Poverty to develop organizations and institutions to benefit their community in East Los Angeles. Two of the key institutions they created were The East Los Angeles Community Union (TELACU), which focused on economic development, and the Chicana Service Action Center (CSAC), which provided job placement for Mexican American women.[11]

TELACU joined the self-determination ethos of the Chicano movement with the community focus of the War on Poverty, following a community-union model similar to that of the WLCAC. As Mexican Americans argued for more participation and representation in the War on Poverty, the UAW (prodded by one of its Mexican American members, Glenn O'Loane, who worked at the same Ford assembly plant in Pico Rivera as Ted Watkins) determined to help create an organization similar to WLCAC in East Los Angeles. Indeed, O'Loane noted the money and assistance the UAW was sending to Watkins and the WLCAC for Watts and asked himself and the UAW, "Why not East LA?" UAW's initial response was a donation of $150, with instructions to develop a community union in the barrios of East LA. In February 1968 Mexican American activists and union leaders joined together to form the East Los Angeles Labor Community Action Committee. The organization advocated self-determination, community organization and participation, and economic development; it would be incorporated officially as TELACU later in 1968. The organization was headed by Esteban Torres, a UAW labor organizer from East Los Angeles who was able to establish trust quickly with the residents of the area. Torres saw his task as building "a community organization that could harness its own economic and social power." His inspiration came, in part, as the result of a trip to Mexico in 1966 with César Chavez and UAW president Walter Reuther. Torres noted the new role labor unions were beginning to play in Mexico and Chavez's success at labor organization with the United Farm Workers. He also believed that L.A.'s power structure treated the Latino residents of East Los Angeles as a colony, when they paid any attention to them at all. In order to counter that, Mexican American residents in East L.A. needed to create their own economic and political power agency. Torres proposed using labor-organizing techniques to deal with poverty in East Los Angeles, connecting labor unionism and the Mexican American civil rights movement to the War on Poverty.[12]

In addition, Torres was deeply influenced by scholars who argued that racial minorities in the United States experienced lives similar to those of subjects of European powers. For these theorists, self-determination was central. Torres reflected this thinking when he wrote: "East Los Angeles, like other Mexican-American communities, is but a colony dependent on outside forces that control the ownership and flow of economic resources. Because of that condition, such communities are rendered helpless to affect the social and political institutions about them. Given the ability to own and control their own economic resources, the community can then reverse the situation by attaining political power which then influences the attitudes of the social and political institutions. Moreover, it allows for eventual control, allowing for self-determination." These, then, were TELACU's goals from the beginning—control of economic and political resources to allow for the self-determination of the Mexican American community of East Los Angeles. Since East L.A. was predominantly Mexican American, TELACU also advocated cultural power. The result would be an economic, political, and cultural powerhouse that would force the Anglo-dominated economic, cultural, and political institutions in Los Angeles, and in the nation, to take notice.[13]

TELACU created its organization like a union organizes plants—each of the twelve barrios in East Los Angeles served as a plant, and each barrio/plant had a representative on TELACU's board. Initially, TELACU faced a cool reception from many in the community. Board chair George Solis later remembered: "We had a real problem in trying to get community acceptance. The people just didn't trust us until they were convinced we were here to help." O'Loane met that same frosty reception in TELACU's early days of existence. He later noted, "We had to assure the people that we weren't a big union movement coming in to take over but we're here to lend our help."[14]

One of TELACU's first efforts at community organization succeeded in the creation of over five hundred new public-housing units. The effort was led by residents of the community determined to improve the housing in the area. In addition, TELACU actively participated in events connected to the Chicano movement, such as the antiwar rally in 1970 at which Rubén Salazar was killed. TELACU staff members had helped plan the march and participated in it.[15]

Reflecting the focus of the War on Poverty, TELACU's first community programs were aimed at youth. They included a summer-camp program under the cosponsorship of the WLCAC, Neighborhood Youth Corps programs, and a reading program for young children. Indeed, O'Loane credited the summer-camp program with making adults more receptive to TELACU and its programs. In addition, TELACU developed job-training programs for teenagers and young adults in concert with the UAW.[16]

Not all of TELACU's service programs were created for youth; some of its job training and other programs focused on adults. Its Social Services Department developed the Comprehensive Employment and Training Act (CETA), On-The-Job Training, Work Experience for Out of School Adults, Senior Citizen Dial-a-Ride, and Senior Citizens Food Cooperative programs. Furthermore, in 1981 TELACU opened a Family Health Center with a sliding-fee scale and community education and outreach services.[17]

TELACU also used its organization to develop Latino political power. In 1972 Torres established the Ad Hoc Committee to Incorporate East Los Angeles (ACTIELA) in an effort to fight the historic underrepresentation of Mexican Americans in Los Angeles city and county government. The measure eventually went down to defeat, 58 percent to 42 percent, in 1974 as the result of divisions within the Mexican American community and some residents' fear of higher taxes. Also, the possible significance of incorporation was never made completely clear to many residents of East Los Angeles, as only 15 percent of the electorate voted. TELACU actively continued to pursue political power and representation for Latinos in Los Angeles. It was vital to the growth of the Democratic Party in East Los Angeles and to growing electoral successes for Latino candidates for city, county, and statewide offices from the 1970s to the present day.[18]

In addition to services, community organization, and political power, the TELACU board determined that in order for the community to survive and have influence, East Los Angeles needed to build a strong economic base. Indeed, early in its existence, TELACU created its organization around four central areas: housing and urban development, economic development, manpower, and social services. As a result, TELACU developed a number of business and economic ventures. Its economic programs included currency exchange, food-stamp distribution, a business-development office, an investment company, the Community Thrift and Loan, the TELACU Community Credit Corporation, the Eastland Leasing Company, the Bank of East Los Angeles, and the East Los Angeles Business Development Center. TELACU established many of these financial companies as a result of inadequate services from traditional banking and credit institutions. For instance, the TELACU Currency Exchange was established to provide efficient and accessible food stamp distribution with bilingual service—something the banks that provided food stamps refused to offer—and the Community Thrift and Loan was created as a solution to the practice of redlining, which prevented many Mexican Americans from being able to obtain home loans. TELACU created each of these agencies to provide economic empowerment for the residents of East Los Angeles and the community as a whole.[19]

It also focused much of its attention in its early years on the construction of affordable housing. At the time of TELACU's origins, no public-housing units had been built in East Los Angeles since World War II. In 1971 TELACU opened its first of several housing projects, a small six-unit complex, the Walter Reuther Villa, named after the labor leader and one of the early supporters of TELACU and the community-union concept. The Reuther Villa housing complex symbolized the type of development TELACU wanted to pursue. Designed, developed, constructed, and managed by Chicanos, the Reuther Villa represented the juncture of the War on Poverty and the Chicano movement.[20]

In fact economic development became the cornerstone of TELACU's holistic approach to community empowerment and self-determination. That process of focusing on a central strategy of community economic development began with an OEO grant in 1971. According to Torres: "for too long, external forces had taken capital out of East Los Angeles. It was owned by outsiders and it was controlled by outsiders. We felt it important to work from within to begin to recoup our own posture as an economic entity and to build capital. Out of that would come the political capital."[21]

In order to control that capital, TELACU transformed abandoned buildings in East Los Angeles into thriving businesses. Perhaps its largest and most successful development has been its conversion of the vacant B. F. Goodrich tire manufacturing plant just off Interstate 5 into a thriving industrial park that employs over 2,000 residents of East Los Angeles. Goodrich had employed about 1,500 workers before it vacated the area in 1975. TELACU's board saw an unprecedented opportunity to reverse the trend of industrial flight from East L.A. and received grant money from the Ford Foundation to purchase the plant in 1977. It also established its own furniture and aquarium companies within the industrial park. TELACU officially assumed ownership of the forty-six-acre site on August 31, 1977, and one year later the park opened with Aaron Brothers Art Mart as its anchor business. The organization's connection to the Chicano movement is noticeable in the park's main building, which includes a large mural depicting Mexican American history. Murals have long been a part of Chicano culture and have been used to portray religious, political, economic, and cultural messages. Through murals, walls and buildings have become "a medium for Latino cultural expression." In addition, TELACU had the old Goodrich tower destroyed on Cinco de Mayo in 1978, a tribute to the Mexican heritage of most of the residents of East L.A.[22]

TELACU has displayed its cultural ethos in a plethora of ways. One of its more elaborate ventures into cultural nationalism was its creation of Tamayo Restaurant in a 1928 Spanish Colonial mansion

The Pride of Our Heritage, or *El Orgullo de Nuestra Herencia,* mural on the front of the TELACU headquarters building in the city of Commerce. Photo by the author, December 2006.

next to TELACU Industrial Park in the City of Commerce. Named after Mexican modernist artist Rufino Tamayo, the restaurant's ambience shouts Mexican pride and culture. The restaurant's walls are covered with an impressive collection of Tamayo's large-scale paintings and tapestries. Traditional Mexican musical concerts greet diners, and Mexican fare—from the traditional to the exotic—sates their palates. The brainchild of TELACU CEO David Lizarraga, the restaurant has served as a Chicano cultural center since 1988, as well as a place of employment for many East L.A. residents.[23]

These cultural icons represent the connection between the origins of TELACU and the Chicano movement. TELACU has maintained the community's cultural pride through the artwork in its offices and at Tamayo Restaurant. Its origins as a Chicano organization also remained central to its programs and ideals; indeed, a 1971 report on its housing-development plans centered on TELACU's roots as a Chicano organization. The report argued that "the Chicano community is presently a powerless minority without true representation at any level of government" and that "the goal of the Chicano Movement, or La Raza, is to rectify this situation by uniting la gente, the people, and assisting them to achieve social equality." The report continued that community organizations such as TELACU are "the only means to articulate the community's needs and the only hope in bringing the necessary programs and resources into the community." Thus, TELACU would serve as the link between the Chicano movement and the War on Poverty.[24]

In November 1972 TELACU entered a new phase of its existence when OEO designated the agency as a community-development corporation (CDC). The comprehensive and coordinated CDC philosophy guided TELACU's approach and programs from that point on. As a CDC, TELACU became a very atypical antipoverty agency. Indeed, as a "quasi-public, semi-private institution," it was able to establish for-profit businesses that provided local jobs. Torres believed a business and economic development component was necessary for TELACU in order to provide true self-determination and economic benefit for the Mexican American residents of East Los Angeles. With a philosophy that approached Booker T. Washington's arguments about black economic development in the late nineteenth-century South, TELACU's leaders, particularly Torres and Lizarraga, believed that Mexican Americans could only truly make an impact nationally if they first focused on economic development in their own communities. Lizarraga explained TELACU's shift towards economic development: "We saw what many other social agencies, and we too, were doing in the community as 'band-aid' solutions. While this was important to relieve the pain, no one was really dealing with the underlying economic problems, especially unemployment. It was at that point that TELACU began to stress economic development, while maintaining some of our successful social programs." Lizarraga also noted that TELACU's goal was "to create an independent economy that will make the community self-sufficient. Unless you start building an economic base, you will always be under the control of outsiders. Our main consideration in TELACU's economic development program is a program of assertive action toward self-sufficiency." Thus, TELACU became a culturally and economically nationalist organization.[25]

In 1975, under Lizarraga's direction, TELACU formulated an overall Master Plan that called for the creation of a central financial center to meet the needs of residents. As the historian John Chávez notes, "radical colonial theory underlay this capitalist master plan." Since traditional financial institutions had taken capital from the inner city and invested it elsewhere, East L.A. needed to create its own community-based financial institutions. No other CDCs at the time focused so heavily on developing financial institutions. On the other hand, no other CDC was "in such a position of powerlessness with relation to local government." The Master Plan focused on using venture-capital funds to create financial institutions that would lend or invest to create employment opportunities for the residents of the community. It included four primary components: a Business Development Office, the TELACU Investment Company, the TELACU Community Credit Corporation and Community Thrift and Loan, and a Bank Investment Strategy.[26]

One of TELACU's earliest economic-development projects established it as a major player in economic and political power battles in East Los Angeles. The project was the rehabilitation of the Maravilla barrio, an area that had become the worst housing project in the community.

The Maravilla housing development came about in part with the assistance of an Economic Development Administration (EDA) grant, which TELACU used to create the "Barrio Housing Plan," this in turn leading to a change in strategy for TELACU, one based on housing development. Torres understood the checkered history of urban renewal and knew that the Maravilla barrio project would have to be carried out differently. The inclusion and participation of the residents, a central precept of the War on Poverty, would be central to the project's success. When the Los Angeles County Housing Authority announced plans to reconstruct Maravilla, TELACU and Casa Maravilla, the latter a social-service organization then led by David Lizarraga, brought together residents to demand participation in the decision-making process. It also demanded that minority firms be given some of the construction contracts. Part of the tedious process included getting social-service agencies and rival gangs in East Los Angeles to agree to work together for the overall benefit of the area residents. Their gang coalition, the Federation of Barrios Unidos, helped assure the completion of TELACU's Maravilla housing project.[27]

This was accomplished in part through the use of community-block meetings and town-hall meetings. For the block meetings, TELACU subdivided East L.A. into fourteen smaller districts. Within each subdivision, a block meeting was held in the home of a resident, where neighbors could discuss the Maravilla project. TELACU workers and members of the Federation of Barrios Unidos went door-to-door to advertise the meetings and encourage residents to attend and participate. Many did— the block meetings averaged twenty to twenty-five residents in attendance. In addition, TELACU staff held town-hall meetings every Thursday in both Spanish and English during October and November of 1972 at the Maravilla Service Center and at Our Lady of Soledad Catholic Church to allow more resident participation. In large part as a result of TELACU's involvement, Nueva Maravilla, completed in December 1974, was constructed with overwhelming community support, providing hundreds of jobs to local residents and significantly improved housing for five hundred families.[28]

Another of TELACU's significant economic-development projects was the revitalization of a fifteen-block portion of the Whittier

Boulevard commercial strip in unincorporated East Los Angeles in the late 1970s through the early 1980s. The project included the destruction of old, deteriorating buildings and businesses and the construction of new businesses, placing an emphasis on the cultural heritage of the area's Mexican American residents. TELACU planned its development of Whittier Boulevard to be like a traditional plaza in Mexico and called their project "El Zocalo." They chose Whittier Boulevard, because it had the highest concentration of commercial activity in East Los Angeles and served as a regional shopping area for Mexican Americans. While the Zocalo plan never completely materialized, the Whittier Boulevard shopping district from Atlantic Boulevard to the Long Beach freeway featured upgraded facades and a new Plaza Colonial shopping area, modeled on the Zocalo idea. TELACU continued to influence the area, both economically and culturally.[29]

TELACU faced criticism over the years for its focus on economic development and operating for-profit corporations. Some of the harshest criticism came from Gloria Molina, one of the founders of CSAC, who had earlier worked for TELACU. Molina later argued that TELACU "violated the trust of the community" by investing outside of East Los Angeles and by profiting personally from some of those ventures. Indeed, in 1982 TELACU was investigated by federal auditors, acting on a tip from a former employee, for fiscal irregularities. The employee charged that TELACU had violated federal jobs-program provisions by having program enrollees work for Democratic Party political candidates. The former employee eventually settled with TELACU, but his accusations helped launch a federal investigation of TELACU's business practices. The thirty-month investigation, during which Lizarraga was indicted but not convicted, resulted in TELACU's refunding the federal government $1 million for improper handling of a rural assistance–program grant. In addition, TELACU board chairman Joe L. Gonzalez was placed on five years' probation for admitting he enrolled in a jobs program and received money for work he never did.[30]

Despite some of its legal entanglements, over the years TELACU became a political power broker in East Los Angeles. Virtually all Latino politicians from East Los Angeles owe their success in part to support from TELACU, which has not been shy about actively participating in the political process through monetary donations to politicians. For instance, TELACU donated over $200,000 to political campaigns in southern California in 2001–2002. To those who criticize TELACU's influence and deep pockets, Lizarraga argues, "We are engaging in the political process. That's the American way."[31]

David Lizarraga himself has served as a lightning rod for many of the organization's critics. Born and raised in East L.A., he was in many ways the perfect candidate to succeed Torres as TELACU president in 1974. Prior to joining TELACU, Lizarraga cut his organizational teeth in the War on Poverty, serving as area coordinator of Teen Post programs in East Los Angeles. He then became founder and executive director of Casa Maravilla, providing social services to gang members and others in need in East Los Angeles. He joined TELACU in 1972, already having an impressive War on Poverty and East Los Angeles résumé. He has now served as TELACU's president for over thirty years; as such, he and his organization have influenced or controlled the outcome of most elections having an impact on East Los Angeles.[32]

One exception to that control occurred in the 1982 California State Assembly race between Gloria Molina and Richard Polanco, the latter also having ties to TELACU. The organization unsuccessfully supported Polanco over Molina, and Molina has not forgotten. Indeed, her assessment of TELACU was that "they became just a greedy, self-serving group of people that, very frankly very few people trusted. The concepts that they began with were good, but I think somewhere along the line, the money really deteriorated a lot of their goals, and their achievements were no longer very beneficial to the community." Clearly, Molina's vision of the purpose of the War on Poverty and community action differed from that of Lizarraga and TELACU. Though both Molina and Lizarraga believed in using War on Poverty programs for community empowerment, they disagreed strongly on how to accomplish that empowerment; Molina advocated more community participation, while Lizarraga and TELACU focused more on economic development.[33]

Richard Martinez, a member of UMAS and the Congress of Mexican-American Unity, also worked at TELACU for over a year. He liked the original idea of cooperatives and "workers owning what they create." He left TELACU, though, as he saw it shifting from workers building and owning their homes to economic development. Like Molina, he saw the shift as a fundamental betrayal of the goals of community action and the Chicano-movement origins of TELACU.[34]

Even some of its critics, however, recognize TELACU's accomplishments. Rodolfo Acuña has argued that "for all of the criticism from people such as myself, the reality is that TELACU is an American institution run by brown people. Its success depends on playing the rules of capitalism and influence-peddling. . . . The gnawing reality is that TELACU would not be as successful if it had played by other than American rules, which at times includes a Taco Bell vision of development and the accumulation of political and economic hegemony."[35]

Others accused TELACU of abandoning the community-action/self-determination aspect of its original mandate and of being disconnected from the people of East Los Angeles, who are supposed to be its primary clients. Indeed, one TELACU board member admitted that the organization "did not want to become a large or mass membership organization, but rather we hoped to provide [economic] assistance to our neglected community." Lizarraga, who has served as TELACU's president since 1974, argued that TELACU fulfilled its mandate through job creation and economic development and by serving as a catalyst for private-sector reinvestment, but he also noted that TELACU needs "to continue to be a catalyst in the community, and to continue to be responsive to the community."[36]

While both TELACU and WLCAC created the community-union model of fighting poverty, their approaches varied to a certain extent. Both were clearly and unreservedly culturally nationalist organizations. Both utilized a holistic strategy, but they had different areas of emphasis. TELACU used more of a top-down approach, focusing primarily on economic development and political and cultural power, and at times it relegated participation to a secondary goal. WLCAC, on the other hand, initially emphasized more community participation from "the bottom up, and the inside out, rather than from the top down and the outside in."[37] Over the years, though, WLCAC became a nonprofit corporation and, like TELACU, shifted toward economic development.

TELACU has changed in at least one other respect. Like WLCAC, it has broadened its base, but in a different way. TELACU has reached out to an ever more diverse Latino population in East Los Angeles and has expanded its economic development outside of East Los Angeles to areas such as San Bernardino, California; San Antonio, Texas; and Washington, D.C. Indeed, TELACU's geographical expansion began early in its life. In 1978 it joined with five other CDCs to form the Hispanic American Coalition for Economic Revitalization (HACER), the concept for which was initiated by the TELACU Community Research Group for information exchange and cooperative projects. In that year TELACU made its first loan to a Chicano-owned business outside East L.A. In doing so, it argued that "these investments are in line with our company policy that assisting any economically or socially disadvantaged group benefits all such groups." By 1980 TELACU was involved, through HACER, in economic-development projects in locations as geographically dispersed as Salinas, San Jose, Las Vegas, Miami, and Yakima, Washington.[38]

Part of the reason for TELACU's success during the 1970s was the expansion of federal support during the decade, especially during the Jimmy Carter administration. CDC funding increased initially in the early 1970s, when Congress—with the support of President Richard Nixon, who believed CDCs would encourage black capitalism—passed Title VII in 1971. But the most significant expansion of the decade occurred during the Carter administration. CDCs appealed to Carter's ideal of local control of resources. During Carter's four years in office, the federal government averaged over $2 billion in annual assistance for CDCs. TELACU, WLCAC, and other CDCs nationwide were able to take advantage of that federal largesse and greatly expand economic development in their communities.[39]

TELACU and WLCAC became CDCs and received federal funding in part because their leadership was male. The increased participation of women in Community Action Programs led one OEO staffer to argue that "the failure to involve men . . . has been the single most important failure of the Poverty Program. But economic development is different. Business is man's work. It promises power and status." As a result, the vast majority of federal money for CDCs went to organizations such as TELACU and WLCAC that were headed by men.[40]

While the Carter years were ones of growth and expanding federal support for CDCs, survival became more difficult for many CDCs during the Ronald Reagan presidency in the 1980s, which witnessed the dissolution of the Community Services Administration and the repeal of Title VII. Reagan-administration budget cuts and policy changes made life for many CDCs impossible, and a number folded. Those that did not collapse—mostly the larger organizations—thrived. With fewer CDCs to compete with for federal funds and demonstrating an ability to obtain funds from sources in addition to the federal government, TELACU expanded its investments and economic development.[41]

By the 1990s TELACU had over $300 million in assets and ranked in the top twenty-five Latino businesses in terms of revenue. In 2005 TELACU Industries had fallen to forty-eighth in the ranking of top Latino businesses by *Hispanic Business*, with earnings of over $130 million, although it ranked fourth nationally among Latino financial corporations. It employed over 1,500 local residents; the businesses it had helped finance and construct employed thousands more. Clearly, it had made an economic impact in East Los Angeles.[42]

TELACU has not been the only CAA in East Los Angeles—indeed, several others have operated in the area over the years, including Cleland House, the East Los Angeles Action Council, Parents Involved in Community Action, United Community Efforts, Inc., and others. But, TELACU has lasted the longest and has had much more of an economic, political, and social impact than any of the others.[43] An article in the *Los Angeles Times* recognized TELACU's significance, arguing that "TELACU might be just another outfit claiming to speak for another place if it didn't have federal sponsorship and venture capital and United Auto Workers funding and Ford Foundation support and a growing supply of homegrown economists, planners, administrators. TELACU might be just another grant-grabber if it hadn't already opened a thrift and loan company within the community, managed two profitable manufacturing companies, run a successful public murals program, [and] launched a biweekly free cultural celebration."[44]

John Chavez, the primary historian of TELACU, argues for its significance because its presence "represents a reassertion of the Mexican Americans' place in Los Angeles and the Southwest, but also integration" and the organization "serves as a model of self-determined and equal participation" in American society and politics. Chavez also extols TELACU for its focus on "the importance of real estate for economic recovery" and on "power based on ownership and control of land." Chavez rightfully asserts that much of Mexican American history has been about land—Mexican control of the lands of the Southwest and the subsequent loss of those lands to the United States. Ever since that loss, Mexicans in the United States have been a people with little control of the land. TELACU has restored some of that control, and in doing so has restored some of the cultural power of Mexican Americans.[45]

WLCAC and TELACU have not solved the problem of poverty, but they have provided an important alternative approach. As both integrative and community-based corporations, they have existed between government and business. In communities ten miles apart, with shared yet separate histories, these community institutions, created by the War on Poverty, arose out of movements for self-determination, cultural identity, and empowerment and became powerful symbols for their respective communities. As they maintained that cultural significance, they also moved toward a more integrative, interracial, inter-ethnic, and inter-regional—yet still community-based—attack against poverty. WLCAC and TELACU also represent the ways in which the shifting boundaries of race shaped the development of the War on Poverty in Los Angeles and the War on Poverty helped mold and alter those racial and cultural boundaries. They suggest that the multiracial character of the American West framed the contours of the War on Poverty in Los Angeles, so that any discussions of the War on Poverty in the West must move beyond the black-white biracial paradigm.[46] Finally, WLCAC and TELACU demonstrate that while there may have been a connection to the civil rights movement in the policy's origins, perhaps a more long-lasting and significant connection to social movements occurred during the implementation of the War on Poverty in communities focused on cultural and economic empowerment—and they demonstrate that the "long war on poverty" is still being fought.

Chapter 6
Empowering La Nueva Chicana
The Chicana Service Action Center

CHICANA ACTIVISTS IN East Los Angeles founded another ethnically distinct antipoverty organization that reflected and challenged the model created by WLCAC and TELACU. They established the Chicana Service Action Center (CSAC) as a Community Action Agency in June 1972 as an affiliate of their Chicana organization Comisión Femenil Mexicana Nacional (CFMN), founded in 1970. The CSAC combined the framework of the War on Poverty and the ideology of a burgeoning Chicana activism to provide services and leadership training for Chicanas in East Los Angeles. The women who founded CSAC were influenced by the Chicano movement. At the same time they desired to establish their own organizations, free from the sexism of the Chicano movement and independent of a women's movement they believed did not adequately address issues of concern to women of color, such as employment and poverty. Instead, they used the framework of the War on Poverty to organize and train women for leadership positions in East Los Angeles and in the Chicano movement. Indeed, Chicana activists used the community-action model of the War on Poverty and the ideology of the Chicano and feminist movements to forge a Chicana antipoverty organization focused on the cultural, economic, and political empowerment of Chicanas in East Los Angeles. The CSAC's goals of bringing War on Poverty services and programs to needy women in East Los Angeles, as well as training women to become leaders in the Mexican American community, demonstrated the malleability of the War on Poverty and its intricate relationship with movements for cultural, economic, political, and gender empowerment.

The CFMN and the Birth of the CSAC

The Chicana Service Action Center was born of the growing Chicano movement. In 1970 Mexican American activists held a National Issues Conference in Sacramento, sponsored by a coalition of statewide Chicano organizations: the GI Forum, LULAC, MAPA, and the Association of Mexican American Educators (AMAE). About thirty Chicanas at the conference met in a women's issues workshop to discuss topics of importance to them, such as abortion, birth control, child care, poverty, Chicano stereotypes, machismo, and Chicana leadership. Some women at the workshop wanted the new organization to focus on welfare rights, but most of those involved were not welfare recipients, so the majority decided to include welfare as *an* issue for the new organization but not *the* issue. This clearly reflected the influence of both the Chicano and the feminist movements as well as the fact that most of the women present were not poor.

The key women involved in these discussions included Francisca Flores, Yolanda Nava, Lilia Aceves, Manuela Banda, Bernice Rincón, and Frances Bojórquez, many of whom had participated actively in Mexican American civil rights organizations. Most of the women at the workshop were married, working women, and the topics of discussion reflected their collective perspective. Prior to the workshop, Flores and a few others drafted a list of discussion topics, including "Women's Rights—What are They? Should Women Run for Public Office? Women and Family: Should Women Work? Should We Support Child Care Centers? Abortions? Feminism: What Does this Mean?" and others. Angered primarily by their exclusion from leadership roles in Mexican American organizations, the women decided that a new Chicana organization was needed, so they created the CFMN in order to organize and train women to assume leadership in the community and to address the key issues they believed were important to Chicanas. The members of the new CFMN wasted no time, quickly passing resolutions advocating for bilingual, bicultural sixteen-hour child-care centers; legalized abortion and birth control; and the creation of a women's antipoverty organization as an alternative to unequal representation in existing community-action agencies such as TELACU.[1]

The resolution establishing the CFMN outlined the reasons for its creation and its purpose:

The effort and work of Chicana/Mexicana women in the Chicano movement is generally obscured because women are not accepted as community leaders, either by the Chicano movement or by the Anglo establishment . . . THEREFORE, in order to terminate exclusion of female leadership in the Chicano/Mexican movement and in the community, be it RESOLVED that a Chicana/Mexican Women's Commission be established at this Conference which will represent women . . . and; That the Comisión direct its efforts to organizing women to assume leadership positions within the Chicano Movement and in community life, and; That the Comisión disseminate news and information regarding the work and achievement of Mexican/Chicana women, and; That the Comisión concern itself in promoting programs which specifically lend themselves to help, assist and promote solutions to female . . . problems and problems confronting the Mexican family . . . VIVA LA CAUSA![2]

The CFMN clearly identified itself from the outset as rooted in both the Chicano movement and feminism.

The CFMN's connection to feminism is reflected in its support of birth control and abortion rights. Yolanda Nava, one of the founders of CFMN, noted that she and her colleagues were well aware of the white feminist movement and translated that movement into Chicanas' issues. According to Nava, the primary motivation behind the creation of CFMN was the founders' belief that Chicanas "were suffering from the double stigma of not only being Mexican American but also being women in the double layer of racism and sexism." While she often served as a bridge to white women's groups, Nava noted that most Chicanas believed the white women's movement had little to say to them.[3]

Flores concurred with Nava. She believed that Chicanas had "always been isolated from the Anglo Women's movement. Our issues do not coincide because I don't think the Anglo will ever really understand. Just as women have to do for women, so Mexicans have to do for Mexicans because they're the ones who know what they want. So women have to fight for their own, and they can only do it by combining with their own."[4]

Flores's statements about Anglo feminists reflected the thinking of many Chicanas in the early 1970s, who felt "consistently marginalized in the Anglo feminist community because of [Chicanas'] critique of [Anglo feminism's] racial/ethnic prejudice and lack of class analysis." According to Elena Olazagasti-Segovia, "for Hispanic women it is very hard to understand why Anglo women are unsatisfied and feel the need to complain. The reaction is not What are they complaining about?, but Why are they complaining at all? Since they belong to the dominant cultural group, they have it made!" Olazagasti-Segovia argued that for Chicanas, "the invitation of Anglo women to join their movement sounds as suspicious as the song of the sirens."[5]

The CFMN, then, represented an effort by Chicana feminists to separate themselves from the mainstream Anglo feminist movement. One of the resolutions passed by that initial group of thirty CFMN members in 1970 noted the organization's dual inspiration from the Chicano and feminist movements: "the effort and work of Chicana/ Mexicana women in the Chicano movement is generally obscured because women are not accepted as community leaders, either by the Chicano movement or by the Anglo establishment."[6] In addition, the CFMN's original goals—to develop Chicana awareness, advocate for Chicana rights, provide leadership training, ensure the welfare of the Chicana community and remain a female-dominated organization— reflected its origins as a Chicana feminist agency.

Like the Chicana movement itself, the CFMN was both feminist and nationalist, resulting from women's politicization based on their activism in the Chicano movement, but also from internal struggles within the movement. Some of those struggles were the result of the subordinate positions of women and the dominant positions of men within Chicano organizations.[7]

Further, Flores argued that the CFMN was organized "to provide a platform for women to use for thinking out their problems, to deal with issues not customarily taken up in regular organizations, and to develop programs around home and family needs."[8] The "regular orga-

nizations" Flores referred to were the Mexican American civil rights
and antipoverty organizations—such as the GI Forum, LULAC, and
TELACU—which were male led and male focused. Flores later remembered about the male-dominated organizations: "they used us; the
men had us doing the work and they couldn't have operated without the
women. Yet, women were never nominated for president, vice president, or any other executive office." The founders of CFMN were
motivated by "the realization that it didn't matter how long we worked
together with the men in MAPA and other organizations, we were not
part of the leadership and they weren't going to allow us to be part of it."
Thus, Flores saw the creation of CFMN partly as "a subconscious attack against women's' auxiliaries" of traditional Mexican American civil
rights organizations.[9]

Francisca Flores: From Civil Rights to the War on Poverty

Flores was quite familiar with "regular" civil rights and civil-liber-
ties organizations. She embraced several throughout her lifetime and,
by 1970, had an impressive résumé of support for liberal/leftist causes.
She had helped Carey McWilliams research *North from Mexico*; had
helped to organize underground screenings of the film *Salt of the
Earth*; had actively participated in the American Civil Liberties Union
(ACLU) and its defense committee for the Sleepy Lagoon defendants;
had joined in the Democratic Minority Conference in the late 1950s;
had founded the League of Mexican American Women and had served
as its chair from 1959 to 1964; and had helped found the Mexican American Political Association (MAPA) in 1960.

Her politicization occurred relatively early in life, when as a young
woman she was hospitalized for ten years (1926–36) for tuberculosis.
During her time recuperating in a sanatorium in San Diego, she met
many veterans of the Mexican Revolution and helped form a group,
Hermanas de la Revolución Mexicana, where women could talk politics. Thus, her education was informal; she possessed no college degree, although as a lifelong learner she took fifty-six credits' worth of
college courses. Flores worked as a medical secretary and an administrative assistant to fund her political activities. Throughout her public
activism, she always advocated for more prominent roles for women. It

was Flores who organized the women's issues workshop at the National Issues Conference in 1970, took a leadership role in CFMN, and became the first executive director of CSAC. Both organizations incorporated the liberal activism, Chicano cultural pride, and feminist ideology that so defined Francisca Flores.[10]

Beginning in the mid-1960s, Flores also edited *Carta Editorial,* an early Mexican American civil rights journal, devoting herself both to the Mexican American cause and to the journal. In a letter to Philip Ortega, a professor at New Mexico State University, she humbly discussed her journal, telling Ortega, "the Carta is still an infant publication and a very poor one. I now carry the burden (which I enjoy) alone. I work in an office to earn a living in order that I might publish the Carta . . . my education quite limited but with a lot of nerve I venture to use a language I hardly know but the only one I can use at all."[11] Flores used the pages of *Carta* to advocate for the causes in which she believed. In one 1963 issue, she discussed the place of Mexican Americans and African Americans in American society, noting that both experienced the shared problem of "race prejudice." Two years later, Flores criticized America's involvement in Vietnam, a view that many younger Mexican Americans would express over the next several years. Flores's editorship of *Carta* demonstrated her fundamental commitment to Mexican American civil rights and presaged the central role of print culture to Chicana feminism later in the 1960s and 1970s.[12]

Throughout her life, Flores maintained a close friendship and correspondence with Graciela Olivarez, a Chicana activist who helped found the National Organization for Women (NOW) in 1966, headed the Arizona Office of Economic Opportunity, and served as director of the Community Services Administration during the Jimmy Carter presidency in the late 1970s. Flores and Olivarez both dedicated themselves to the cause and corresponded regularly during the early 1960s about Mexican American civil rights efforts. In a letter written to Flores just days after President John F. Kennedy's assassination in November 1963, Olivarez complained about the lack of progress Mexican Americans were making in civil rights. She told Flores, "in spite of all the noise we have been making in the southwest, none of it has reached Washington and so we can spend the rest of the year and next making

A young Francisca Flores at the tuberculosis sanatorium in San Diego in the 1930s. Her politicization began there. Courtesy CFMN-CEMA, University of California Santa Barbara Special Collections Library, Box 48, Folder 5.

speeches, noises, holding conventions and everything else but . . . we are just spinning our wheels. . . . We need to do a lot of work in the field of orienting and training. We are way behind the Negro." Olivarez concluded her letter talking about creating an interracial "democratic coalition of the southwest," including blacks, Mexican Americans, and Jews. Her dream of a democratic, interracial coalition never quite came to fruition, despite her efforts.[13]

Later that year in a letter to Flores, Olivarez continued to express her frustration over the lack of progress by Mexican Americans, complaining that "nuestra gente esta muy verde cuando de politica se trata y me lastima ver como somos la burla de los demas" (our people are very green when it comes to politics and it hurts me to see some of us deceive the rest).[14] The following year, the lack of attention to Mexican American civil rights issues remained a source of irritation to Olivarez. She complained to Flores that the U.S. Commission on Civil Rights investigators had been in Los Angeles "and got absolutely nowhere with their investigation. After my plea and my 'ruegos' [requests] to the Commission two years ago and getting Father Hesburgh,[15] one of the Commissioners to become interested in the plight of the Mexicano, they send out investigators who can't get any information because everyone keeps saying that all is fine with the Mexicanos."[16] Two years later, Flores herself testified before the California State Advisory Committee to the U.S. Commission on Civil Rights when it returned to Los Angeles to hear grievances of Mexican Americans. Thus, in the mid-1960s both Flores and Olivarez remained frustrated at the lack of movement by Mexican Americans and the federal government on civil rights issues for Americans of Mexican descent.[17]

Flores and Olivarez both made the transition from Mexican American civil rights activism to involvement in the War on Poverty, but at different times. Olivarez was the first of the two to move to antipoverty programs. In October 1964, two months after President Lyndon Johnson signed the Economic Opportunity Act, Olivarez wrote Flores, "I've become a consultant to the poverty people." She added, "your name and address with a high recommendation from yours truly was given to the VISTA people."[18] Over the next few years, Olivarez became consumed with War on Poverty activities and duties, and she and others continued to encourage Flores's involvement. In 1965 Olivarez was appointed to the Advisory Council for the Office of Economic Opportunity and served as executive secretary of the National Conference on Poverty in the Southwest. She wrote to Flores, inviting her to attend the conference and participate more actively in the War on Poverty.[19]

Several other War on Poverty officials contacted Flores over the next few years to attempt to entice her into more active involvement with antipoverty programs. The director of the Job Corps Center for Women asked Flores to be on the center's Advisory Committee, and the director of the UCLA Upward Bound asked the same of her. The coordinator of the Conference on Women in the War on Poverty in 1967 invited Flores to participate, and she did so. At that conference she met William Crook, the director of VISTA, who later asked her to join that agency. She agreed, instead, to serve on the UCLA Upward Bound Advisory Committee. Other OEO officials contacted Flores for information on Mexican American civil rights groups and for her participation in various conferences and agencies. From the mid- to late 1960s, Flores remained in regular contact with Olivarez and other officials of various War on Poverty agencies. By 1970 she was intimately familiar with the programs and policies of the OEO and the War on Poverty and saw the antipoverty program as a way to extend her involvement in civil rights efforts. Indeed, both Flores and Olivarez demonstrate the fundamental and intricate connection between the struggle for Mexican American civil rights, feminism, and community organizations of the War on Poverty.[20]

The CSAC and Job Training for Chicanas

Under Flores's leadership and to achieve its goals, particularly to ensure the welfare of Chicanas, the CFMN determined to create a Chicana antipoverty organization. It applied for and received a fifty-thousand-dollar grant from the Department of Labor Manpower Administration, which had been given some of OEO's War on Poverty funding powers by the Nixon administration in order to create a Community Action Agency to assist low-income Chicanas. Initially funded as a one-year demonstration project, the CFMN opened the Chicana Service Action Center on Boyle Street in East Los Angeles in August 1972.[21]

The CFMN's original proposal for the creation of CSAC noted the existence of government programs and social-service agencies designed to aid the unemployed and underemployed but argued that "little, if any, emphasis has been placed on the needs of women . . . Child Care, women's health needs in family planning, general health, education, and employment are the felt needs of women within the disadvantaged community. In view of these needs, coupled with the lack of mobility, as well as a lack of English language skills, it is proposed to establish a women's center in the Mexican American community." In addition, the proposal listed as CSAC's objectives identifying women who needed services, advocating for women's needs, developing new employment opportunities for Chicana women, and publishing a newsletter to disseminate information. Finally, the proposal argued that "center staff must be trained to understand the problems of all women, and in particular Chicanas." The CSAC clearly reflected the confluence of feminism, Chicana activism, and the community-action aspect of the War on Poverty.[22]

CSAC leaders, like the planners for the national War on Poverty, focused much of their efforts on job training. In 1970, 15 percent of Chicanas in Los Angeles were unemployed, and their median income was less than one-third that of Chicanos. In addition, 25 percent of Chicanas in Los Angeles worked in service positions, 27 percent worked in clerical jobs, and only 5 percent received paychecks for professional employment. The fact that 42 percent of Mexican American families in Los Angeles County headed by women were living at or below the poverty level highlighted the importance of well-paid employment for Chicanas. Early indications at CSAC reinforced what its leaders already believed about the importance of job training. Over 50 percent of Chicanas who came to CSAC were unskilled or untrained women under the age of thirty, and most were high-school dropouts and single mothers.[23]

Much of the ideology behind the job-training programs of the CSAC reflected the opportunity theory of sociologists Lloyd Ohlin and Richard Cloward, which had informed the creation of the War on Poverty.[24] CSAC leaders believed a number of obstacles existed for Mexican American women that kept them in poverty and prevented their economic success. Those obstacles included racism, sexism, communication barriers, a lack of vocational skills, and a lack of knowledge of job-interviewing techniques. Indeed, one of CSAC's early pamphlets about its job-training programs noted that its services were "provided to help participants overcome personal and environmental barriers which affect their training and/or employability." Anna Nieto Gomez, CSAC's special projects director, argued that for Chicanas with language skill problems, "opportunities in the labor market are primarily menial and found only where large numbers of people in the same position are employed, i.e., canneries [and] garment factories." To CSAC advocates, then, job training and removing obstacles to Chicana employment were central to its strategy. Nieto Gomez best summarized this approach when she wrote: "the Chicana Service Action Center is calling attention to the Educational training needs of the Chicana in order to better her economic opportunities in the job market and in education. We feel it is vitally important that educators, woman-manpower experts, and employers become more aware of the real socioeconomic picture of the Mexican-American woman in order to more adequately serve her."[25]

CSAC developed three methods of providing job training to the women who came through its doors. The first, titled "womanpower services" (with language clearly reflecting the influence of feminism) provided mock interviews and a thirty-day job-orientation class. The second, work experience, gave enrollees twenty-one weeks of employment in a nonprofit agency. The third, classroom training, provided women with educational training to help them receive their GED. Language comprised a key part of job training at CSAC. Many of the agency's clients, especially early in its existence, possessed limited knowledge of English. For those women, information on financial-aid opportunities and job listings was provided in Spanish. CSAC geared each of these three job-training methods to make its clients more employable by removing obstacles to their employment—appropriate education, language, and training. It represented the opportunity theory in action.[26]

One challenge that CSAC leaders noted early on was the inadequacy of training programs for Chicanas age thirty-five and over. It was logistically impossible for CSAC, in its first year, to establish any special training for women in this age group that would prepare them to enter existing manpower programs, because those programs required English fluency. CSAC responded to the challenge by establishing its own language program in its second year of existence.[27]

CSAC monthly reports reveal more information about the types of women receiving assistance through the agency. In November 1973 CSAC staff members counseled fifty women in person. Most CSAC clients were young—over half were between the ages of sixteen to thirty, 28 percent were ages thirty to forty-five, and only 16 percent were forty-five to sixty-five years old. Those percentages remained similar throughout much of CSAC's history. For instance, in December 1973, 58 percent of clients were sixteen to thirty, 29 percent were thirty to forty-five, and 13 percent were forty-five to sixty-five. In addition, in November 70 percent of CSAC clients were single, separated, or divorced, and 65 percent of single women had children. The numbers in December 1974 remained similar. In that month 67 percent of CSAC's clients were single, separated, or divorced. In addition, 30 percent had an eighth-grade education or less. In other words, a majority of CSAC clients were young, single women with children, some of whom lacked educational and/or language skills. Indeed, the report noted that the large number of single women with children "indicates the imperative need for adequate facilities for child care."[28]

From August 1973 to May 1974, CSAC had placed forty-six women in outside job-training programs. Those programs trained CSAC clients for clerical positions; English as a second language positions; and jobs as computer programmers, electronic assemblers, nurses' aides, and teachers' aides. During that same period, CSAC staffers had placed eighty-two women directly in jobs, including twelve women in educational positions, twelve in industrial jobs, thirty-eight in clerical positions, twelve in service jobs, and twenty in social-service occupations. CSAC funneled its clients to jobs with companies such as Southern California Edison, Rockwell, Prudential Insurance, IBM, Safeway, CBS, and United Way. CSAC counselors also successfully placed clients in jobs in banks, schools, department stores, hospitals, and government agencies such as the Social Security Administration, the Los Angeles County Probation Office, and

A CSAC staffer and a client. Most women who used CSAC's job-training programs were young and single. Photo courtesy CFMN-CEMA, University of California, Santa Barbara, Special Collections Library, Box 48, Folder 1.

the Greater Los Angeles Community Action Agency (GLACAA). In addition to those direct placements in jobs and job-training programs, CSAC staffers referred 213 women to job-training programs and 532 women to jobs, while also providing general employment counseling to 102 additional women. During that ten-month period, over 1,000 women received services through CSAC.[29]

Wilma Perez and Linda Martinez represent two examples of young Chicanas who benefited from CSAC's job-training programs. Perez, a divorced twenty-two-year-old mother with a three-year-old child, enrolled in CSAC's thirty-day job-preparation class in hopes of finding permanent employment. Within days after completing the orientation, Perez was hired as the new program director at the YWCA in Lincoln Heights.[30]

Linda Martinez dropped out of college during her second year in order to have a baby. She soon found herself a single mother on welfare.

CSAC clients practice their clerical skills as part of one of the agency's job training programs. Photo courtesy CFMN-CEMA, University of California, Santa Barbara, Special Collections Library, Box 48, Folder 7.

When her newborn was three months old, she enrolled in one of CSAC's job-training and placement programs while her daughter attended the agency's child-care center. She hoped to find a job, but instead she found —thanks to the job counselors at CSAC—a career. A few months after arriving at CSAC, the twenty-one-year-old landed a well-paid position as a math aide at Aerospace Corporation in El Segundo. She also reentered college to complete her degree in math. Perez and Martinez serve as examples of how CSAC could work to improve the lives of unemployed, poor Chicanas.[31]

When asked by a newspaper reporter to describe the training CSAC provided its clients, Francisca Flores discussed aptitude tests, résumé writing, interviewing techniques, and communication skills. But, she added, "We try to give them strength in terms of self-confidence. We place them where they'll be able to move upward on their own. . . . We have to make the women feel good about themselves. . . .

We hope that will hold them through what comes next. . . . It's a long haul."[32] This clearly demonstrates that Flores and the CSAC leadership saw empowerment as central to its job-training programs.

In addition to training women for clerical and service positions, CSAC also initiated programs that stretched the generally accepted boundaries of women's employment. In 1975 it began a women's managerial manpower-training program that prepared women to be executives and administrators. A year later the agency began a women's preapprenticeship program that trained women for nontraditional employment in construction, electrical work, and other skilled manual trades. Each of these programs reflected CSAC's connection to feminism and its emphasis on expanding possibilities and opportunities for women.[33]

CSAC leaders met some resistance to their agency. In 1974 the organization applied for a nine-hundred-thousand-dollar Comprehensive Employment and Training Act (CETA) grant from the Los Angeles County CETA Appeals Committee. The committee rejected most of CSAC's proposal, funding only 10 percent of its request for counseling and supportive manpower services instead of a comprehensive CETA training program. County staff argued that Mexican American women did not need job training services, because they did not need jobs. Staff members also reasoned that CSAC's program would discriminate, since it would serve only Chicanas. One male member of the CETA Appeals Committee derisively referred to the CSAC board members present as "those feminists."[34]

Flores and the CSAC board fought for their proposal. Throughout the fall of 1974, Flores badgered CETA officials at the local, state, and federal levels. Her letters combated claims that Mexican American women did not need the services and that CSAC's program would not provide any new services. She also rallied CFMN members behind her cause. In early December she penned a letter to all CFMN members asking for their support of CSAC's battle for CETA funds, arguing that "the Chicana Service Action Center is presently fighting for its program." Finally, in late December, Flores received word that her efforts had prevailed—CSAC would receive its CETA funding.[35]

Passed by Congress in 1973, CETA became the most significant federal jobs program in the 1970s. In 1977 and 1978 President Jimmy

Carter signed legislation doubling the number of public-service jobs funded through CETA and greatly expanding the funding for job-training programs. For community organizations throughout the nation that, like CSAC, focused most of their energy and resources on job training, CETA was vital. Throughout the 1970s CETA funds helped provide job training and placement for thousands of women through CSAC and millions nationally through other community organizations. The Reagan administration, however, killed CETA in 1982 as part of its effort to reduce big government, much of which was done at the expense of the poor and unemployed in America.[36]

In the 1970s, however, CETA funding remained a vital source, and CSAC used some of its CETA funding to join forces with other job-training agencies to create the Los Angeles Resource Center for Low-income Women. Established in 1976, this jointly controlled CETA agency served low-income women interested in seeking nontraditional employment. It reflected one of many avenues through which CSAC attempted to train and refer clients to jobs.[37]

As they trained Chicanas for employment, CSAC leaders recognized another need these women had—child care. Most of the women, like Linda Martinez, who came to CSAC, did not have access to affordable child care, which represented another obstacle to their employment. Chicana leaders had identified this issue as central when they first organized CFMN in 1970. When they broached the subject to the National Issues Conference as a whole, the men at the conference rebuffed the notion. But the Chicana leadership remained committed to the idea, and in 1973 CSAC applied for and received a grant from the California State Department of Education and the Los Angeles City Community Development Agency for the creation of two day-care centers whose primary purpose was to provide child care so that mothers could find better jobs and further their education.[38]

In December of that year, CSAC's Centro de Niños opened two centers, one in the East Los Angeles Maravilla Housing Project and the other in Echo Park, a predominantly Mexican American community just north of downtown Los Angeles near Dodger Stadium. Sandra Serrano Sewell served as the director of the centers, which were governed by the CSAC's Board of Directors and an Advisory Council, composed of parents and representatives of the community who were experts in the field of early childhood education. In addition to providing free child care for working mothers and bilingual and culturally positive early childhood education for their children, it also provided educational programs in the evenings. Chicana mothers attended seminars on parenthood, gang prevention, child development, narcotics, and drug abuse.[39]

In a development that reflected both its grounding in feminism and its intention to open up blocked opportunities, the CSAC opened two Battered Women's Shelters and a Family Crisis Center in 1978. As the organization and its clientele grew during the mid-1970s, CSAC employees and administrators recognized the problems of domestic violence and family unrest and saw them as other impediments to employment and the economic emancipation of Chicanas. Funded through the Los Angeles County Community Development Program's Community Action Agency funds, CSAC created its domestic-violence shelters with the hopes of serving up to sixty women and ninety children. CSAC allowed women to stay at the Battered Women's Shelters for any period from twenty-four hours to thirty days.[40]

Over the course of the 1970s, the CSAC expanded in the number of clients it served, the number and type of programs it offered, and the number of its locations. From 1973 to 1977, CSAC served over fifteen thousand women in five centers in East Los Angeles, Van Nuys, West Los Angeles, Lincoln Heights, and Bell Gardens. All of these locations were in heavily Mexican American neighborhoods, reflecting the cultural empowerment focus of the Chicana movement. In addition to offering job and educational training and child-care and domestic-counseling services, CSAC offered nutrition workshops, leadership workshops, and a Chicana Businesswomen's Conference. It also became involved in issues of political empowerment in the 1970s including voter-registration drives, the "Las Mujeres for Brown" campaign for the California gubernatorial election in 1976, opposition to Alan Bakke's anti-affirmative-action lawsuit, and participation in marches in support of the Equal Rights Amendment.[41]

The CSAC: Training Chicana Leaders

Another important goal of CSAC from its inception was leadership training. Not only did CSAC administrators want to train women for jobs, they wanted to prepare them to be business, economic, and political leaders. Inspired by both the Chicano and the feminist movements, the founders of CFMN and CSAC argued that Chicana leaders were necessary to attain real economic and political power for Chicanas —and CSAC's leadership-training program successfully did that. A number of administrators, employees, and clients at CSAC became leaders in business, labor, and politics. For instance, Lilia Aceves, an early founder of CSAC, left the agency in 1973 to become project coordinator for the City of Los Angeles Office of Urban Development; Leticia Quezada, a former employee, became the Los Angeles Unified School District's first Latina school-board member; and Yolanda Nava was appointed to the California State Attorney General's Task Force on Women's Rights and later in the 1970s became a news anchorwoman for the CBS affiliate in Sacramento.

Gloria Molina serves as the primary example of Chicana leadership emanating from CSAC. Molina used her experience as the first chairwoman of CSAC to become more active in political advocacy on issues of import to Chicanas. In addition to her involvement in CFMN and CSAC, she worked as a job counselor at TELACU in 1971 and as an instructor at the East Los Angeles Skills Center in 1972. Her role as chairwoman of CSAC further politicized her thinking. She first became directly involved in politics when she became the administrative assistant for assemblyman Art Torres in 1974. During that period, she also sat on the California State Advisory Committee to the U.S. Commission on Civil Rights and served as chair of the commission's Women's Rights Committee. She then served as chief deputy to Willie Brown, Speaker of the California State Assembly, and as deputy in the Office of Presidential Personnel in the Jimmy Carter White House. Many Chicanas saw her election to the California State Assembly in 1982 as an example of the success of the leadership focus of CSAC. Indeed, following her election to the State Assembly, Molina wrote Gloria Moreno Wycoff, "I am so very proud of the women that took on this grand challenge. I am especially proud of the Comisión women. They were great."[42]

Molina's 1982 election also represented a break with the Mexican American political establishment, which had strong ties to TELACU. Molina's opponent was Richard Polanco, who had credentials similar to those of Molina, including connections to TELACU. The only real difference between the two was gender. When the all-male Mexican American political leadership decided on Polanco as their candidate, Molina decided to challenge the network. In the process she splintered that machine to an extent, gaining the support of congressman Ed Roybal and assemblyman Art Torres, and shattered the perceptions of what a Chicana could accomplish. The campaign increased Molina's distaste for TELACU, whose focus on development she observed with a wary eye. She believed TELACU had lost its original War on Poverty goal of community involvement. This division was further demonstrated in Molina's campaign for county supervisor in 1991. Again, she was opposed by TELACU and its supporters, and this time their candidate was Art Torres, who had supported Molina in 1982. Molina won the election, including a clear majority of votes in East L.A. Her victory signified the political clout of Chicanas and the success of the political and leadership training of the CSAC. It also demonstrated the clear connection between Mexican American civil rights struggles, government liberalism, feminism, and the War on Poverty.[43]

This focus on training Chicana leaders represents a distinct style of leadership by the women of CSAC. Clearly, Flores, Molina, and the other leaders of the organization served as more than "bridge leaders" of the black freedom movement described by Belinda Robnett. While they did at times serve as bridges between the ordinary unemployed clients of CSAC and Chicano political leadership, more often they provided the political and economic leadership themselves. Indeed, their collective style of leadership also challenges Karen Sacks's description of "center women" who sustain women's networks but allow male leaders to be the public spokespeople of an organization, cause, or movement. Flores, Molina, Nava, Nieto Gomez, and others in CSAC, through their writings, public testimony, press conferences, and political activism, worked as more than sustainers of networks; they were, loudly and clearly, the spokeswomen for the cause of Chicanas in Los Angeles. Perhaps they most closely resemble Nancy Naples's description of activist mothering—using social activism to address the needs of the community.[44]

The CSAC and Cultural and Gender Empowerment

Central to all of CSAC's programs and goals from its inception was the notion of cultural empowerment. Indeed, CSAC leaders chose a logo that reflected the organization's Chicana focus, featuring a clearly Native Mexican woman's face with a large, broad nose and thick lips surrounded by Native Mexican symbols. The CFMN logo also featured a Native Mexican, but its image was in profile, with a flower in her hair. Both logos demonstrated the organizations' Chicano and feminist roots and mission.[45]

CSAC newsletters served as one of the key avenues through which the CSAC promoted the ideology of the Chicana movement. The group's organizers made this abundantly clear through the title of the cover-page article in the first issue of the agency's newsletter: "The Emancipation of the Mujer." With the words "emancipation" and "mujer," CSAC organizers demonstrated that the agency concerned the cultural, political, and economic freedom of Chicanas. Articles in other newsletters told stories of Mexico, informed readers on issues of concern to Chicanas, and highlighted the accomplishments of women of Mexican descent.[46]

The CSAC newsletters represented a central aspect of the Chicana movement—print culture. A number of Chicana publications, including *Regeneración,* founded by Francisca Flores in 1970, *Hijas de Cuauhtémoc,* founded by students at California State University, Long Beach, in 1971, and *Encuentro Femenil,* founded by Anna Nieto Gomez in 1973, emerged during this period as Chicana outlets for artistic expression, scholarly analysis, and political and cultural exhortation. Focusing on issues of "collective self-knowledge" and "collective self-determination," the CSAC newsletters served as "organizing tools" for the Chicana movement and as one of the "inventive forms of print intervention [that] helped to constitute and document new forms of Chicana insurgency during this period."[47]

A poem published in the May 25, 1973, CSAC newsletter is a prime example of the cultural-empowerment focus of CSAC and its centrality in the organization's newsletters. Written by Viola Correa, it addresses the political, cultural, and economic empowerment that was central to the philosophy of CSAC.

La Nueva Chicana

Hey!
See that lady protesting against injustice,
    Es mi mama
That girl in the brown beret,
The one teaching the children
    She's my hermana
Over there fasting with the migrants
    Es mi tia.

These are the women who worry, pray, iron,
And cook chile y tortillas.
The lady with the forgiving eyes
And the gentle smile,
Listen to her shout!
She knows what hardship is
All about.
The establishment calls her
A radical militant.
The newspapers read she is
A dangerous subversive.
They label her to condemn her.
By the FBI she's called
A big problem.
In Aztlán we call her
    La Nueva Chicana! [48]

The poem describes a woman's world, or perhaps more accurately, a Chicana woman's world. It contains no explicit male characters—they are only implied. It is a world where women provide the nutritional, economic, cultural, and political sustenance, one where women are empowered. It is the world of La Nueva Chicana. The poem serves as a clarion call to Chicanas that they have a history not only of "women's work," but also of protest and power. In the poem Chicanas have a history not only of economic hardship, but of economic and political action. The poem, much like the CSAC, brings together the community-action aspect of the War on Poverty, the culturally nationalist ethos of the Chicano movement, and the gendered analysis of feminism.

Correa's poem reflected a new term that Chicanas had begun to use to identify themselves. Initially, Chicanas in the late 1960s to early 1970s used the slogan "Chicana Primero" to urge themselves "to take pride in their cultural heritage and to reject the women's liberation movement." Women used the new term, "La Nueva Chicana," to emphasize the "combination of the strengths of their womanhood with the strengths of their cultural heritage." In addition, the term reflected the "dynamic relationship between gender and ethnicity." The printing of Correa's poem in the CSAC newsletter demonstrated the organization's central identity as a feminist and culturally nationalist War on Poverty agency.[49]

Like print culture, murals also served as an avenue for Chicana cultural expression and empowerment, as the mural on the TELACU building demonstrates. One CSAC program reflected that form of cultural communication. In 1978 CSAC began a job program that hired its clients to paint murals in Los Angeles schools, focusing on those in Chicano neighborhoods. A group of Chicana artists completed the first project—a 230-foot-long mural along the hallway of the administration building at Humphrey Avenue Elementary School. The mural portrayed women actively at work as doctors, astronauts, and other professionals. CSAC's goals for the project included beautifying the school, providing jobs for low-income women, creating an opportunity for cultural empowerment for the women employees and the children at the school, and portraying Chicanas as positive, active agents in society. It made a lasting impression on the students. One teacher noted, "the students have it so ingrained that women can't do certain kinds of jobs, the mural really makes them think. . . . [the murals] portray the future for students at the school. They look at the women and say 'Gee, I didn't know women could do that.'" When completed, the mural represented another vehicle through which the CSAC connected the War on Poverty with movements for cultural and gender empowerment.[50]

As part of its campaign for cultural and economic empowerment, the CSAC actively championed the cause of Chicanas in the media as well. In March 1975 Anna Nieto Gomez wrote a letter to all Chicanos in the media in Los Angeles, arguing for the inclusion of Chicanas in 50 percent of all programs on television. Nieto Gomez later reported to Flores on the positive response to her letter, also telling her, "we have begun to identify the Chicana Service Action Center as an advocate of mujeres in the community."[51]

The CSAC incorporated themes of cultural empowerment into their employment-training programs as well. In July 1974 the CSAC began a summer Chicana Communications Skills Development Program at East Los Angeles College for young women ages fourteen to seventeen. Nieto Gomez and others at the CSAC designed the Neighborhood Youth Corps (NYC) program "to develop communication skills through a Chicana studies curriculum." Nieto Gomez geared the guest speakers and research assignments "to provide the girls with a good image of themselves as women and as Chicanas." The program focused on economic empowerment by preparing the participants for interviews and employment tests. The CSAC noted that the NYC program's goals were "to promote a better self image for those Chicanas entering the labor force; to prepare the Chicana for job placement; to develop communication skills." Nieto Gomez noted that the CSAC created the program "with the help of Chicana volunteers involved in developing curriculum on Chicana history, health, welfare, education, and employment."[52] CSAC leaders clearly envisioned their employment-training programs not just as opportunities for economic empowerment for their clients, but also as a source of cultural empowerment, with CSAC programs providing job and cultural training. CSAC leaders shaped the War on Poverty to fit their needs of cultural and gender empowerment and used the programs of the War on Poverty to shape the Chicana movement in East Los Angeles.

This focus on the Chicana movement and activism caused some controversy within the CSAC. Indeed, within a few years of CSAC's founding, the CFMN and CSAC boards split, and CSAC incorporated and became an independent agency. That decision was made in part because Flores and Corrine Sánchez, CSAC's deputy director at the time, wanted to expand the agency's services to other Mexican American communities in Los Angeles, which meant independent incorporation. Flores later mourned the loss of the direct connection to CFMN, noting that "the Center always felt the loss of the Comisión membership; we could have gone to the membership to build an economic base. The organization could have been a strong source of support. Comisión, for their own reasons, did not give the Center the time it needed. They had moved into the women's movement, Chicana issues, and politics."[53] Indeed, while preparing to write a history of CSAC, Flores handwrote the following notes about this CFMN-CSAC conflict: "Project moved faster than organization—fights between Comisión and CSAC Board— CSAC became incorporated on its own—Comisión tried to prevent this." Flores went on to describe the years of 1975 to 1977 as a period of "great animosity" between CFMN and CSAC.[54]

Flores's tenure as CSAC director was not without other tension. Flores demanded much of herself and her employees, some of whom resented her for it. After complaints from some staff members about long working hours and unpaid lunches, Flores agreed in 1977 to set an office schedule of nine to five, with a paid lunch. Her ambivalence toward this new policy showed in her memo to staff members, where she noted that "continued tardiness on the part of staff will jeopardize this new time schedule, and might cause a reversal to the previous schedule."[55]

Workplace tensions and conflict continued to fester at CSAC and led to Flores's submitting her resignation in November 1981. In 1982, with Sophia Esparza as CSAC's new executive director, an internal CSAC report noted "serious problems" including "a high degree of staff turnover and high absenteeism," which, the report argued, reflected "burn-out and low staff morale." The report also noted that the agency remained in a "constant state of flux" due to "overwork and underpayment" as well as "job uncertainty." It concluded that those issues needed to be addressed, "otherwise the corporation will be stagnant and suffer long term." The report deemed it "vital that management by objective become standard operating procedure for Chicana Service Action Center. This will aid employees in feeling an important part of the organization's survival. We need not accept our history of staffing patterns as part of the norm in community based organizations." Indeed, Esparza's report concluded: "Chicana Service Action Center has in the last year seen a significant transition which I will term the 'Managerial Revolution.'" Flores's departure had been a key element in that transition.[56]

The CFMN and CSAC, though, never completely severed connections, and Flores retained an affiliation with both organizations. Indeed, the CFMN honored her at their Twentieth Anniversary Gala in 1990 for her contributions to their organization and to Chicanas as a whole. Several dignitaries feted her with laudatory speeches, and the CFMN presented her with a plaque emblazoned with the CFMN logo.[57]

The honors CFMN bestowed on Flores were well deserved. Not only had she played a significant role in CFMN and CSAC, but she also became an important player in the War on Poverty in Los Angeles outside of CSAC. In addition to her extensive involvement in Mexican American civil rights organizations in the 1950s and 1960s, Flores was often included in organizations that came together to address issues of poverty in the city. In 1973 she served on the committee to hire the community coordinator for the Greater Los Angeles Community Action Agency (GLACAA). The following year she joined the board of the Los Angeles County Opportunities Industrialization Center, an antipoverty industrial employment agency, along with Ted Watkins, Ed Roybal, Gus Hawkins, Lilia Aceves, and Gilbert Lindsay.[58] But, of course, Flores's signal contributions were in relation to CFMN and CSAC. Indeed, it is fair to argue that without her, neither of those organizations would have come into existence. She was the original driving force behind both of them, which served as the culmination of her lifelong pursuit of economic, social, and cultural empowerment of Chicanas. In the process she helped a new generation of Chicana leaders, who broke the boundaries of women's roles in politics and society.

In 1997 thousands of people gathered at the swank Regent Biltmore Hotel in downtown Los Angeles to celebrate the twenty-fifth anniversary of the CSAC, a thriving, active remnant of the War on Poverty. By the time of this anniversary, the organization that had started with the coming together of thirty women at a Chicano issues conference in 1970 had served well over one hundred thousand Chicanas, who had received job training, sent their children to day care at the Centro de Niños, been housed in the Battered Women's Shelter, or received counseling at the Family Crisis Center. And above all, one hundred thousand women had been instructed in the ways of "La Nueva Chicana."[59]

This party, though, took place without Francisca Flores, who had passed away a year earlier from complications resulting from a stroke at age eighty-three. Several of her former CFMN and CSAC colleagues— Lilia Aceves, Anna Nieto Gomez, Gloria Wycoff, Corinne Sánchez, and Sandy Serrano Sewell—spoke fondly of their mentor at her funeral. Her memorial, attended by a few hundred, was held at the CSAC, an organization that she had been primarily responsible for creating. At the time of her death, the CSAC served approximately twenty-five thousand women each year.[60]

The continued existence and growth of the CSAC demonstrated that the War on Poverty did not end in the 1970s. Instead, the War on Poverty morphed and reshaped itself, in East Los Angeles, as a result of its confluence with the cultural nationalist ethos of the Chicano move- ment and the insurgence of feminism. As Mexican American men be- came Chicanos and Mexican American women became Chicanas, racial, cultural, economic, and gendered identities merged, evolved, and chal- lenged traditional definitions. The CSAC's story, much like Annelise Or- leck's story of Operation Life in Las Vegas, also suggests that—at least in certain cases—the War on Poverty worked. In both these cases, women of color were able to shape the War on Poverty to fill some of their eco- nomic, cultural, and political needs. Chicanas in Los Angeles, like black women in Las Vegas, used the framework of the War on Poverty to create a racial/ethnic and gender-based organization that promoted the training and employment of empowered Chicana women. The women of the CSAC directly linked the Chicano movement, feminism, and the War on Poverty.[61]

The CSAC's story, along with studies by Orleck, Greene, and Rhonda Williams, also demonstrates the centrality of gender and wom- en's organizations to the struggle against poverty nationally. Indeed, women's neighborhood organizations became a vibrant part of the War on Poverty in the late 1960s and early 1970s. As in Las Vegas, Durham, Baltimore, and other cities across the United States, women of color in

Los Angeles intentionally created their own antipoverty organization, free of male control. They believed women had specific economic needs that could be met only through a women's organization.[62]

Finally, the CSAC story also suggests that the War on Poverty continues to be waged; the "long war on poverty" has extended well beyond the 1960s and 1970s. For more than thirty years in Los Angeles, Chicana women have ensured that the War on Poverty has provided almost two hundred thousand Chicanas with jobs; job training; child care; leadership training; education; shelter from abuse; and cultural, political, and economic empowerment. Clearly, the War on Poverty has, indeed, empowered "La Nueva Chicana."

Epilogue

IN THE KEN BURNS DOCUMENTARY series *The Civil War,* the historian Barbara Fields argues that the battle for freedom begun during that war is ongoing and could still be lost.[1] In many ways I see the War on Poverty as part of that ongoing struggle for freedom. During the 1960s and 1970s in Los Angeles, African Americans, Chicanos, and Chicanas used the framework of the War on Poverty—through organizations such as the WLCAC, TELACU, and CSAC—to further define the meaning of freedom for themselves and their communities.

Certainly, African Americans and Mexican Americans saw the War on Poverty as a possible vehicle for their further inclusion in American society. However, as they realized the roadblocks to that inclusion and as their racial-freedom struggles shifted away from inclusion and incorporation and toward nationalism and community control, racially separate community organizations made sense to many African Americans and Chicanos in Los Angeles. The Watts revolt was central to that shift. Individuals and organizations that had been willing to work toward inclusion in YOB and EYOA shifted toward separatism after Watts. The EYOA and, in particular, NAPP showed how interracialism was no longer a valid strategy for using the War on Poverty framework. Although attempts at interracialism continued throughout the 1960s and 1970s, most African Americans and Chicanos shifted toward newly formed, community-controlled War on Poverty organizations to further define their freedom.

It was through racial, cultural, and economic nationalism that blacks and Chicanos in Los Angeles created permanent, community-controlled institutions that provided services to the poor; developed housing and business centers in racially distinct neighborhoods; and celebrated race, culture, and gender. The War on Poverty gave black power, Chicano power, and feminism in Los Angeles a context that they would not otherwise have had. It also provided a structure, through the maximum feasible participation of the poor and through community action, for the creation of black power, Chicano, and feminist anti-poverty organizations.

In his speech to the Congress of African Peoples in 1970, black nationalist author Amiri Baraka told the gathered crowd: "You must control everything in the community that needs to be controlled. Anything of value; any kind of anti-poverty program . . . anything that brings money, resources into your community, you should control it."[2] That philosophy of community control and ownership permeated the operations of the WLCAC, TELACU, and CSAC. Clearly influenced by the ideas of what Jeffrey Ogbar calls "radical ethnic nationalism," the organizations used the structure of the War on Poverty to further those ideas in their respective communities.[3]

All three of those organizations were also community based. Since Los Angeles was highly segregated when the War on Poverty was created, neighborhoods and communities such as Watts, South Central Los Angeles, and East Los Angeles were racially distinctive. When the three culturally nationalist organizations formed in the mid- to late 1960s, they naturally coalesced around those particular communities. Those three organizations are now permanent, influential institutions in Los Angeles, although none are not quite as exclusively community focused as they were initially. TELACU now invests in and develops properties in poor neighborhoods throughout the United States; CSAC offices and centers are located in various parts of Los Angeles; and WLCAC serves a community with a rapidly expanding majority-Latino population. At the time of their formation, though, the WLCAC, TELACU, and CSAC created their own definitions of race and used those definitions to forge their own weapons—whether economic, cultural, or political—in the War on Poverty. Those definitions and weapons have evolved over time, but each agency continues to use its own understanding of race and power to continue the fight against poverty in the twenty-first century.

Significantly, two of the organizations discussed in this book, CSAC and NAPP, were organizations that were exclusively or predominantly women's organizations. In both employment and program delivery, these organizations directly or indirectly attracted women. NAPP and CSAC reflected the significant number of women's neighborhood organizations within the national Community Action Program, which at times was accused by critics of being dominated by women's organizations.[4] Clearly, the women involved in the War on Poverty both nationally and in Los Angeles, particularly those in CSAC, saw women's poverty as a unique problem that was best addressed by a women's organization.

Importantly, this is not a story simply about organizations. It concerns ordinary people who saw the War on Poverty as an ideal vehicle for the extension of American democracy, for an expansion of the "long civil rights movement." Whether they came through the black or Mexican American civil rights movements, feminism, or black or brown power movements, particular individuals shaped the War on Poverty in Los Angeles. As a result, those organizations are distinct. Individuals used their own cultural, economic, and political experiences as well as the milieu of the times to create a myriad of antipoverty wars in Los Angeles. Ted Watkins tapped into his years as a labor organizer and civil rights activist, relating those experiences to black nationalism and forging WLCAC as a culturally and economically nationalist antipoverty organization in Watts. Esteban Torres and David Lizarraga used their union and community-agency experience to shape TELACU into an economic-development based, culturally nationalist antipoverty organization in East Los Angeles. Francisca Flores, Anna Nieto Gomez, Yolanda Nava, Gloria Molina, and others used their experience in Mexican American civil rights organizations and women's rights groups to develop a uniquely Chicana feminist agency fighting poverty in East L.A.

The War on Poverty in Los Angeles, then, was shaped by individuals who were influenced by the ideology of the black freedom struggle and Mexican American civil rights efforts. They used that ideology to shape their War on Poverty agencies into culturally and economically nationalist organizations, while concomitantly using the War on Poverty to further those movements for cultural and economic empowerment. In the process WLCAC, TELACU, and CSAC created permanent and lasting changes in the geographical, economic, and cultural landscape of Los Angeles. The continued presence and activism of those organizations and the permanency of their contributions to the economy, culture, and politics of Los Angeles support the idea of a "long war on poverty." The War on Poverty did not end in the 1970s; instead, it continues through organizations such as the WLCAC, TELACU, and CSAC. From the *El Orgullo de Nuestra Herencia* mural on the front of the TELACU building, to WLCAC's housing developments and its involvement in the Watts Summer Festival, to CSAC's culturally positive images of Chicana women, these organizations demonstrate the many ways in which the War on Poverty helped remap Los Angeles racially, culturally, and economically. Indeed, the organizations that emerged from the War on Poverty helped reshape the city's racial, cultural, and economic boundaries.

Some of the racial and cultural boundaries in Los Angeles are shifting again. In 2001 Antonio Villaraigosa failed in his attempt to become the city's first Latino mayor in well over a century. He lost in large part because of his poor showing among black voters, who gave 80 percent of their votes to Villaraigosa's opponent, James Hahn, whose father, Kenneth Hahn, had championed black causes on the Los Angeles County Board of Supervisors for decades. In addition to supporting Hahn because of his family legacy, many blacks voted against Villaraigosa due to their fear and suspicion of Latinos. Key black politicians such as representative Maxine Waters feared that if Villaraigosa won, it would cost blacks political power.[5]

Four years later, the story had a different ending, indicating some of the possibilities of interracial cooperation and coalition. In 2005 Villaraigosa was elected mayor, this time with significant support from certain sectors of the black community (including endorsements from representative Waters and city councilman Bernard Parks, who were angry with Hahn for his ousting of Parks from the office of chief of police). Indeed, Villaraigosa doubled his portion of the black vote from 20 to 40 percent. At the same time many blacks opposed Villaraigosa's election, with a majority still voting for Hahn, and Villaraigosa's campaign at times exacerbated tensions between blacks and Latinos.[6]

This has not been the only recent instance of increasing tensions. In the spring of 2005, black and Latino students at Jefferson High School in South Central Los Angeles battled during lunchtime, and interracial fights broke out at other Los Angeles–area high schools in the days afterward. The fight at Jefferson High School seems to have been related to changing racial and geographic boundaries. In the 1960s Jefferson High was a predominantly black high school; by 2005 it was 92 percent Latino.[7]

Those statistics reflect what one scholar has called the "Latinoization" of Los Angeles. By 1990 Latinos made up a near majority of the population in South Central, which led to "escalating conflict" between blacks and Latinos in the area over schools, jobs, and housing. By 2000 the Latino population in South Central constituted over 50 percent of the area's total and 47 percent of the entire population of the city of Los Angeles, while African Americans constituted only 11 percent of the city's population.[8]

Much of that increase in the Latino population in the city has been due to immigration; indeed, in 2000, 41 percent of residents of Los Angeles had been born in other countries. Those increasing numbers and the movement of new Latino immigrants into some traditionally African American neighborhoods have added to the interracial conflict and tension over housing and jobs. Many of the new Latino immigrants are from nations other than Mexico, which has led to tensions between Mexican American residents and the newer immigrants from Central and South America. Definitions of race are again being contested in Los Angeles, and nationally as well.[9]

As Angelenos, and Americans in general, attempt to make sense of these new conflicts, perhaps we would do well to remember the history of the War on Poverty in the 1960s and 1970s. It was a time when ordinary residents used the framework of the War on Poverty to challenge the racial and gendered status quo in an attempt to define their economic, cultural, and political freedom. It was a time when people of color used the long histories of their communities' challenges to racial discrimination and segregation, reshaping ideas and organizations to try to make a better life for themselves and others in their neighborhoods and communities. It was a time when what it meant to be black and what it meant to be Mexican American, male or female, changed. It seems that we have entered another time of changing definitions and evolving boundaries of race in the multiracial City of the Angels and in the nation as a whole.

Abbreviations

The following abbreviations for manuscript collections and newspapers are used throughout the notes.

CAP-NARA   Records of the Community Action Program, RG 381, National Archives, College Park, Maryland

CFLA-UCLA   Comisión Femenil de Los Angeles Papers, University of California, Los Angeles, Chicano Studies Research Center

CFMN-CEMA   Comisión Femenil Mexicana Nacional Archives Collection, California Ethnic and Multicultural Archives, University of California, Santa Barbara, Special Collections Library

CSF   California State University, Fullerton, Special Collections Library

CSLA   California State University, Los Angeles, Special Collections Library

LACA   Los Angeles City Archives, Records Management Division, City Clerk's Office, Los Angeles

LACBOS   Los Angeles County Board of Supervisors Records, Board of Supervisors Office, Los Angeles

LAHE   *Los Angeles Herald Examiner*

LAS   *Los Angeles Sentinel*

LAT   *Los Angeles Times*

LBJL   Lyndon Baines Johnson Presidential Library, Austin, Texas

NAACPW   Western Regional Files, National Association for the Advancement of Colored People collection, Library of Congress, photocopy version

SCL   Southern California Library for Social Studies and Research, Los Angeles

UCLA   Special Collections, Young Research Library, University of California, Los Angeles

USC   California Social Welfare Archives, Specialized Libraries and Archival Collections, University of Southern California, Los Angeles

WHCF   White House Central Files, Lyndon Baines Johnson Presidential Library, Austin, Texas

Notes

Introduction

1. "History of Comisión Femenil de Los Angeles, Feb. 1983," Box 1, Folder 6, CLFA-UCLA; Molina interview.

2. Patrick McGreevy and Jessica Gresko, "Renewed Focus on Watts' Lessons: At the Flashpoint of the 1965 Riots," *LAT*, Aug. 12, 2005, B1.

3. John R. Chávez, *Eastside Landmark*, 127–31.

4. Johnson, *Public Papers*, vol.1, 114.

5. Lyndon Baines Johnson, "Message on Poverty," March 16, 1964, WHCF, SP2-3/1964/WE Poverty Message, LBJL.

6. Johnson, *Public Papers*, vol. 1, 125.

7. Califano, *Triumph and Tragedy*, 59–64.

8. Studies of Los Angeles were thin until the 1990s witnessed a flowering of scholarship on the City of Angels. Some scholars referred to this growing field as the "Los Angeles school." This scholarship has presented Los Angeles as both exceptional and unique among American cities and also as "exemplary" or "paradigmatic" of the late twentieth-century and early twenty-first-century American city. This study of the War on Poverty in Los Angeles fits well into both descriptions of the Los Angeles school. See, for example, Dear, Schockman, and Hise, *Rethinking Los Angeles*; Scott and Soja, *The City*; and Davis, *City of Quartz*.

9. See White, "Race Relations," 396–97. On the multiracial origins of Los Angeles, see Lawrence B. De Graaf and Quintard Taylor, "Introduction," and Jack D. Forbes, "The Early African Heritage of California," in De Graaf, Mulroy, and Taylor, *Seeking El Dorado*.

10. Interestingly, most histories of race in Los Angeles have focused on one particular racial group—blacks, Latinos, or Asians. On African Americans in Los Angeles, see, for example, Flamming, *Bound for Freedom,* and Sides, *L.A. City Limits*. On Latinos, see Acuña, *A Community Under Siege*; Ernesto Chávez, *¡Mi Raza Primero!*; Romo, *East Los Angeles*; and Sánchez, *Becoming Mexican American.* The few interracial studies of Los Angeles include Kurashige, "Transforming Los Angeles"; Leonard, "Interest of All Races" in De Graaf, Mulroy, and Taylor, *Seeking El Dorado*; Leonard, *The Battle for Los Angeles*; and Yu and Chang, *Multiethnic Coalition Building*.

11. Piven and Cloward, *Regulating the Poor.*

12. Davies, *From Opportunity to Entitlement.*

13. Krainz, *Delivering Aid*; Orleck, *Storming Caesar's Palace*; Naples, *Grassroots Warriors*; and Greene, *Our Separate Ways.*

14. Quadagno, *The Color of Welfare*; Russell, *Economics, Bureaucracy, and Race.*

15. Asian Americans were not prominent in the War on Poverty in Los Angeles in the 1960s. Less than 5 percent of the poor in Los Angeles in the 1960s were Asian American. That number increased with the influx of immigrants from Southeast Asia in the late 1970s and 1980s. By the 1990s, residents of Asian and Pacific Islander descent constituted 10 percent of the city's population. See Pitt and Pitt, *Los Angeles A to Z.*

16. This phrase is borrowed from Robert Self's excellent study of African Americans in Oakland. See Self, *American Babylon.*

17. For the purposes of this study, I found George Mariscal's definition of cultural nationalism most useful: "the strategic deployment of key features" of a racial/ethnic group's "history and culture in order to fashion individual and collective subjects capable of asserting agency and demanding self-determination." See Marsical, *Brown-Eyed Children,* 45.

18. Some examples include Moynihan, *Maximum Feasible Misunderstanding*; Greenstone and Peterson, *Race and Authority*; and Katz, *The Undeserving Poor.*

19. Hall, "The Long Civil Rights Movement."

20. Matthew Whitaker found similar interracial tensions with limited cooperation between blacks and Mexican Americans in his study of the black freedom movement in Phoenix, another multiracial city in the American West. See Whitaker, *Race Work,* esp. chap. 6. For examples of interracial cooperation during the 1960s and 1970s, see Mariscal, *Brown-Eyed Children,* esp. chap. 5. For a less optimistic view of black/brown relations, see Vaca, *The Presumed Alliance.*

21. I first used this term at the "War on Poverty and Grassroots Struggles for Racial and Economic Justice" conference at the Miller Center for Public Affairs at the University of Virginia in November 2007. The term was inspired by Jacquelyn Dowd Hall's use of the term "long civil rights movement," by the scholarship of Annelise Orleck and others, and by the discussions at the conference.

Chapter 1

Epigraph: Quoted in Pitt and Pitt, *Los Angeles A to Z,* 351–52.

1. Ibid., 263.

2. Banfield, *Big City Politics,* 80–83.

3. Pitt and Pitt, *Los Angeles A to Z,* 397–98.

4. Greenstone and Peterson, *Race and Authority,* 30.

5. Much of the information on Yorty's career is from Bollens and Geyer, *Yorty.* See also McGirr, *Suburban Warriors,* 199. The quote regarding LBJ is from *LAT,* June 29, 1960. The quote regarding JFK is from Yorty, "Ask the Mayor" interview, 100.

6. Davis, *City of Quartz,* 126–27; and Banfield, *Big City Politics,* 84–85. On Yorty's racial ideology and targeting of Bradley, see Payne and Ratzan, *Tom Bradley,* 90–96.

7. Dorothy L. Moore, Secretary to Yorty, to Marvin Watson, June 19, 1967, WHCF, LG/Los Angeles, LBJL.

8. Yorty to LBJ, June 8, 1964, WHCF, LG/Los Angeles, Box 9, LBJL.

9. De Graaf, "The City of Black Angels," 328; Taylor, *In Search of the Racial Frontier,* 300–301.

10. Pitt and Pitt, *Los Angeles A to Z,* 5, 40, 303, 306, 413.

11. For an insightful look at the growth of the Los Angeles NAACP in the 1940s, see Sides, "Rethinking Black Migration," 200–204.

12. Quote is from Greenstone and Peterson, *Race and Authority,* 29. See also Cohen, "The Context of the Curfew Area," in *The Los Angeles Riots,* 63; Scoble, "Negro Politics in Los Angeles," 661–62; and Sonenshein, *Politics in Black and White,* 141–42.

13. Quote is from Thomas G. Neusom, president of the Los Angeles NAACP, "Annual Report of the President," December 18, 1955, Folder "OA Reports—Branch, Los Angeles, 1946–57," NAACPW. For an insightful look at the growth of the Los Angeles NAACP in the 1940s, see Sides, "Rethinking Black Migration," 200–204. For information on the decline of the Los Angeles NAACP, see Horne, *Fire This Time,* 171–77. For more on the general class distinctions in the African American community, see Gaines, *Uplifting the Race.* For an analysis of class divisions in an African American community in another western city, see Quintard Taylor's excellent study, *Forging of a Black Community.* For an informative account of the NAACP in the 1930s that focuses on the hesitancy of the largely middle-class organization to use direct action, see Bates, "New Crowd Challenges the Agenda," 340–77.

14. "Citizens Mobilize to Fight Prop. 14," *LAS,* Aug. 6, 1964, I, 1, col. 5; Sonenshein, *Politics in Black and White,* 36, 41; Horne, *Fire This Time,* 46.

15. Sonenshein, *Politics in Black and White,* 36–37.

16. Ibid., 40–46; Payne and Ratzan, *Tom Bradley,* 58–61.

17. Sonenshein, *Politics in Black and White,* 56–57. Josh Sides makes this point about class differences in *L.A. City Limits,* as does Douglas Flamming in *Bound for Freedom.* Quintard Taylor and James Grossman make the point about old-timers versus newcomers in Seattle and Chicago, respectively; see Taylor, *Forging of a Black Community,* and Grossman, *Land of Hope.* On African American suburbanization, see Wiese, *Places of Their Own.*

18. Quotes are from Payne and Ratzan, *Tom Bradley,* 65. See also Sonenshein, *Politics in Black and White,* 243.

19. When Caucasians began arriving in significant numbers in the late nineteenth century, blacks were unable to find housing in Los Angeles and were forced to live in Watts, then a separate city. By 1926 blacks were ready to take control of the

city government of Watts, but the KKK convinced the city of Los Angeles to annex Watts, thus removing black political control from the area where most blacks lived. See Pitt and Pitt, *Los Angeles A to Z*, 537.

20. For a discussion on Proposition 14, although one focused primarily on Berkeley, see Rorabaugh, *Berkeley at War*, 57–60. On housing discrimination in Los Angeles, see Horne, *Fire This Time*, 26–36, and "Citizens Mobilize to Fight Prop 14," *LAS*, Aug. 6, 1964, I, 1.

21. Horne, *Fire This Time*, 241; Clark and Hopkins, *A Relevant War Against Poverty*, 168.

22. Cloward and Ohlin, *Delinquency and Opportunity*. Cloward and Ohlin's opportunity theory would also serve as the intellectual underpinning of the War on Poverty. See also Knapp and Polk, *Scouting the War on Poverty*, 67–68; Sugarman interview.

23. Marshall, *Politics of Participation in Poverty*, 14; Scudder and Beam, *Twenty Billion Dollar Challenge*, 26; Gorman, *Kefauver*, 197–98; "An Inter-Agency Approach to Increasing Youth Opportunities," Yorty Collection, 1962 (2 of 2), Box C-1007, LACA; "Descriptive Statement: Structure and Objectives of the Youth Opportunities Board of Greater Los Angeles," Yorty Collection, 1961–63 (1 of 2), Box C-1007, Projects, Programs, etc., LACA.

24. Goe to Yorty, March 22, 1962, Yorty Collection, 1962 (1 of 2), Box C-1007, LACA.

25. Joint Powers Agreement, April 3, 1962, City Council File #107082, and "Descriptive Statement: Structure and Objectives of the Youth Opportunities Board of Greater Los Angeles," Yorty Collection, Box C-1007, both LACA; OEO press release, Nov. 25, 1964, FG 11–15, OEO, LBJL; Youth Opportunities Board, *Expanding Opportunities for Youth*, 2–3.

26. Marshall, *Politics of Participation in Poverty*, 15; Clark and Hopkins, *A Relevant War Against Poverty*, 93; "UL Opens Watts Office," *LAS*, Aug. 12, 1964, 17A.

27. C. Erwin Piper, City Administrative Officer to Mayor Samuel Yorty and the State, County and Federal Affairs Committee of the City Council, Los Angeles City Council File #122706, LACA.

28. "Poverty War," *LAS*, Aug. 27, 1964, 6A, col. 1.

29. "Bradley Initiates Antipoverty Move," *LAS*, Aug. 27, 1964, A11, col. 1.

30. Quote is from Tyler, "Black Radicalism in Southern California," 98. See also LAAFSNC Minutes, Dec. 17, 1964, and LAAFSNC Minutes, Oct. 22, 1964, both EYOA Records, Box 3, USC; Greenstone and Peterson, *Race and Authority*, 31; Marshall, *Politics of Participation in Poverty*, 15.

31. Walter Jenkins, Special Assistant to the President to Mayor Sam Yorty, 28 September 1964, WHCF, WE 9, LBJL; Greenstone and Peterson, *Race and Authority*, 140–42.

32. "U.S. Grants $2.7 Million to L.A. Poverty Fight," *LAS*, Dec. 3, 1964, A4;

Lisle C. Carter to Bill Moyers, Aug. 21, 1965, WHCF, FG 11–15, OEO, LBJL; Payne and Ratzan, *Tom Bradley*, 70.

33. Marshall, *Politics of Participation in Poverty*, 15.

34. Sam Hamerman, Chair, YOB, and Joseph L. Wyatt, Jr., President, EOF, to L. E. Timberlake, President, City Council, Feb. 11, 1965, Los Angeles City Council File #122706, LACA; YOB, "The War Against Poverty in Los Angeles, April 1965," EYOA Records, Box 3, USC; Hawkins to William Bassett, LA County AFL-CIO, June 7, 1965, Hawkins Papers, UCLA.

35. Mayor Sam Yorty to City Council, April 22, 1965, Los Angeles City Council File #122706, LACA.

36. Tyler, "Black Radicalism," 94.

37. Mayor Sam Yorty of City Council, April 22, 1965, Los Angeles City Council File #122706, LACA.

38. Horne, *Fire This Time*, 51–52.

39. William J. Williams, Congressional Field Director for Congressman Augustus F. Hawkins, to CAPC Members, April 1, 1965, Hawkins Papers, Collection #1642, Box 91, "Anti-Poverty Programs, Misc." folder, UCLA.

40. All quotes except the final one are from Williams to CAPC members. Final quote is from "Rev. Brookins Blasts Mayor," *LAS*, May 6, 1965, A1, 3. See also "War on Poverty Status Pointed Out by Hawkins," *LAS*, July 22, 1965, 2D, col. 4; Marshall, *Politics of Participation in Poverty*, 15–16; Acuña, "A Community Under Siege," 131–32; Gillis Long to Larry O'Brien, Aug. 30, 1965, WHCF, Box 25, "HU2/ST5 Aug. 24, 1965–November 1965," LBJL. It was at this time that Yorty started a file on Brookins, highlighting his "connections" to the left. See Watts Disturbances, Box C-1925, Yorty Collection, LACA.

41. J. Alfred Cannon, "Anti-Poverty Pitfalls," *LAS*, June 27, 1965, 6A, col. 1; Hawkins to Fred Hayes, OEO Associate Director of Community Action Programs, June 22, 1965, Hawkins Papers, UCLA.

42. Paul Weeks, "Poverty War—More Shouting Than Shooting," *LAT*, June 13, 1965, F1, 2.

43. "Leaders Reject Mayor's Alternative to Poverty Board," *LAS*, June 3, 1965, A1, 3.

44. Gus Hawkins, "Crisis in the War on Poverty," *LAS*, June 10, 1965, D3; "Poverty Unity Needed," editorial, *LAS*, June 10, 1965, 6A; "War on Poverty Status Pointed Out by Hawkins," *LAS*, June 11, 1965, D2; "No Solution Seen for Poverty Program Bog," *LAS*, July 1, 1965, A1, D5.

45. Joint Power Agreement, Proposal, July 8, 1965, Los Angeles City Council File #107082, Supplement #10, LACA.

46. City Council Minutes, July 8, 1965, Los Angeles City Council File #104020, Supplement #14, LACA.

47. Ibid.

48. Yorty to LBJ, Sept. 2, 1964, WHCF, Box 9, "LG/Los Angeles," LBJL.

49. James S. Mize, Chief Deputy of the Board of Supervisors, to Mayor Sam Yorty, July 15, 1965, Los Angeles City Council File #107082, Supplement #10, LACA; "Mass Poverty Demonstrations," *LAS,* July 15, 1965, A1.

50. "King Airs Views," *LAS,* July 15, 1965, 6A, col. 1; "32-member Poverty Board Backed by King," *LAS,* July 15, 1965, A1, col. 2.

51. "Mass Poverty Demonstrations," *LAS,* July 15, 1965, A1, col. 1.

52. "Mills Backed on Poverty by Pastors; Debate Recall," *LAS,* July 22, 1965, A1, A11.

53. Paul Weeks, "Poor Wait Outside in Poverty War," *LAT,* Aug. 11, 1965, II-1; Jack Jones, "Anti-Poverty Hearing Praised and Criticized," *LAT,* Aug. 11, 1965, I-3, 20; "Views on Poverty Aired," *LAS,* Aug. 12, 1965, A1.

54. Bill Lane, "The Inside Story," *LAS,* Aug. 11, 1965, A8.

Chapter 2

1. Branch, *At Canaan's Edge,* 284; Horne, *Fire This Time,* 3, 54–55; FBI Report—"Racial Riot—Los Angeles, CA," Aug. 17, 1965, *Civil Rights During the Johnson Administration, 1963–1969,* Reel 6, WHCF; Viorst, *Fire in the Streets,* 307–42; Bullock, *Watts,* 33–34.

2. "Police-Minority Group Relations in Los Angeles and the San Francisco Bay Area," Report of the California Advisory Committee to the United States Commission on Civil Rights, Aug. 1963; "Chief Parker Accused of Being 'Anti-Negro,'" *LAT,* June 12, 1962, I-24; Sonenshein, *Politics in Black and White,* 40; Bollens and Geyer, *Yorty,* 150; Tyler, "Black Radicalism in Southern California," 155.

3. Blauner, "Whitewash over Watts," 176–77.

4. Quote is from CORE press release, June 4, 1964, Box C-1006, Yorty Collection, LACA. See also Charles E. Brown, "CORE, Yorty Confab Set For Friday," *LAS,* Jan. 28, 1965. Parker would stay in office, with Yorty's support, until his death in 1966.

5. George Goodman, "Wider Scope Seen for Poverty Bill," *LAS,* Sept. 13, 1964, A1; Bollens and Geyer, *Yorty,* 153; Samuel Yorty interview by Joe B. Frantz, 15.

6. See Sears and McConahay, "The Politics of Discontent," 437.

7. Tyler, "Black Radicalism in Southern California," 7.

8. State of California, Department of Industrial Relations, Division of Labor Statistics and Research, *Negroes and Mexican Americans in South and East Los Angeles,* San Francisco, July 1966.

9. W. E. B. Du Bois Club of Los Angeles, "The Fire This Time," Nov. 1965, Southern California Library for Social Studies and Research, Los Angeles; Ron Ridenour et al., "The Fire This Time: The W. E. B. Du Bois Club's View of the Explosion in South Los Angeles," Nov. 1965, pp. 1–3, in folder, "Los Angeles Pamphlets—Watts," SCL; Los Angeles Branch NAACP Press Release, Aug. 18, 1965, NAACP Records, Part 27, Series D, Reel 4.

10. Horne, *Fire This Time,* 341.

11. Louis Martin to John Barley and Cliff Carter, Aug. 23, 1965, *Civil Rights During the Johnson Administration,* Reel 6, WHCF.

12. Hawkins to Ramsey Clark, Oct. 10, 1965, Hawkins Papers, UCLA.

13. Remarks of Augustus F. Hawkins to the McCone Commission, Sept. 20, 1965, Hawkins Papers, Box 91, UCLA.

14. Jesse Unruh to Valenti, Aug. 18, 1965, WHCF, HU2/St5, Box 30, "HU2/ST5 Oct. 12, 1965–April 14, 1966," LBJL.

15. George Murphy, telegram to Shriver, in Murphy Press Release, Aug. 17, 1965, Yorty Collection, Box D25, "OEO," LACA.

16. Shriver to Moyers, Aug. 18, 1965, Moyers Files, Box 56, "Office of Economic Opportunity (1 of 2)," LBJL; "A Dispute Over Blame for the Los Angeles Riots," *U.S. News and World Report* 59 (Aug. 30, 1965), 16; Horne, *Fire This Time,* 290.

17. Yorty to Senator Murphy in Murphy Press Release, Aug. 17, 1965, Yorty Collection, Box D25, "OEO," LACA.

18. Shriver to Senator George Murphy, September 9, 1965, Yorty Collection, Box D25, "OEO," LACA; Bollens and Geyer, *Yorty,* 152.

19. Yorty interview by Joe B. Franz, 15–16.

20. David O. Sears, "Political Attitude," 700.

21. J. Stanley Sanders, interview for Watts '65 Oral History Project, Oct. 2, 1990, SCL.

22. *LAS,* Aug. 19, 1965; see also Richard Meyer, "A Child of the Watts Riots," *LAT,* Aug. 10, 1980.

23. Shriver to Califano, Aug. 23, 1965, *Civil Rights During the Johnson Administration,* Reel 6, WHCF; Califano and Lee White to LBJ, Aug. 24, 1965, FG 11–15, OEO, Aug. 1, 1965–Nov. 17, 1965, LBJL; McCone Commission Report, in Fogelson, *Mass Violence in America,* 8; "Report of the President's Task Force on the Los Angeles Riots."

24. Ernest C. Friesen, Jr., to Lawrence Levine, Oct. 26, 1965, WHCF, Box 9, "LG-Los Angeles," LBJL; Jim Reese to Bill Becker, Sept. 2, 1965, Mervyn Dymally Papers, Box 1, CSLA.

25. "Report of the President's Task Force on the Los Angeles Riots," 23. The term "racial nationalism" is from Gary Gerstle's brilliant *American Crucible.*

26. The experience of blacks in Los Angeles apparently reflected the experience of blacks in other cities. According to Kenneth Clark and Jeanette Hopkins, civil rights organizations in several major cities were not strong in poor neighborhoods and focused on racial segregation, not poverty. See Clark and Hopkins, *A Relevant War Against Poverty,* 167–68. For more on the various forms of black nationalism and the Nation of Islam, see Ogbar, *Black Power,* and Joseph, *Waiting 'Til the Midnight Hour.*

27. Joseph, *Waiting 'Til the Midnight Hour,* 123; Branch, *At Canaan's Edge,* 296; Van DeBurg, *New Day in Babylon,* 1–10, 19.

28. Quote regarding middle-class black leaders is from "Interview of Persons Arrested," 1965, Box 6, 12a (8), McCone Papers, quoted in Horne, *Fire This Time*, 209. Quote regarding churches is in Horne, *Fire This Time*, 50–51. See also Horne, *Fire This Time*, 105–106, 126; Bullock, *Watts*, 55–56. For information on Nation of Islam activities in Los Angeles, see Branch, *Pillar of Fire*, esp. chap. 1; and Cohen and Murphy, *Burn, Baby, Burn!*, 249.

29. "Report of the President's Task Force on the Los Angeles Riots," 43.

30. Saul Alinsky interview by Kevin O'Connell, Nov. 30, 1965, Box 8, 18-C, McCone papers, quoted in Horne, *Fire This Time*, 172.

31. Quoted in William J. Raspberry, "Ghetto Tragedy—No Leadership," *San Francisco Chronicle*, Aug. 21, 1965.

32. Quoted in Cohen and Murphy, *Burn, Baby, Burn!*, 10.

33. Quoted in *New York Times*, Aug. 29, 1965, 24.

34. "When the Poor are Powerless," *New Republic*, Sept. 4, 1965, 7.

35. Sonenshein, *Politics in Black and White*, 72,n73; Branch, *At Canaan's Edge*, 294.

36. "Rally for Freedom in Support of the Birmingham Movement" flyer, Box 20, Folder 12—"Negro Affairs and Organizations" folder, Roybal Papers, CSLA; "Rev. King in Rallies Sunday," *LAS*, June 14, 1962, A1, 3; "Yorty Cites King During Local Visit," *LAS*, March 4, 1965, A8.

37. Dick West and Paul Weeks, "Dr. King Hears Watts Protests Over Heckling," *LAT*, Aug. 19, 1965, I-3, 28; Horne, *Fire This Time*, 105–106, 183; Branch, *At Canaan's Edge*, 296.

38. Erwin Baker and Bob Jackson, "King Assailed by Yorty After Stormy Meeting," *LAT*, Aug. 20, 1965, I-1, 3, 26; Lee White to LBJ, Aug. 20, 1965, *Civil Rights During the Johnson Administration*, Reel 14, WHCF; Horne, *Fire This Time*, 183; Branch, *At Canaan's Edge*, 298; *LAT*, Aug. 20, 1965.

39. West and Weeks, *LAT*, Aug. 19, 1965; "King Criticizes Yorty," *San Francisco Chronicle*, Aug. 21, 1965.

40. Lee White to LBJ, Aug. 20, 1965, Lee White Papers, Box 6, LBJL. For a slightly different interpretation of King's visit, one that emphasizes the centrality of economic justice to King's thinking, see the brilliant Thomas F. Jackson, *From Civil Rights to Human Rights*, esp. 240–44.

41. LBJ phone call to MLK, 5:10 P.M. Aug. 20, 1965 at 8578, Audiotape WH 6508.07, LBJL.

42. Jackson, *From Civil Rights to Human Rights*, 240–44; Garrow, *Bearing the Cross*, 439.

43. Ralph, *Northern Protest*, 1–7, 38; Davies, *From Opportunity to Entitlement*, 127, 239–40. Importantly, it was immediately after the riots that the Student Nonviolent Coordinating Committee (SNCC), which would soon remove "nonviolent" from its name, announced that it would shift its civil rights fight from the South and begin to make economic demands. See "SNCC Shifts Civil Rights Fight to Northern Cities, Article Reports," *LAS*, Aug. 19, 1965, 10B.

44. Joseph Califano, quoted in Kearns, *Lyndon Johnson and the American Dream,* 305.

45. Ibid., 62–63.

46. Collins to LBJ, n.d., WHCF, Box 25, "HU2/ST5 Aug. 24, 1965–Sept. 11, 1965," LBJL. (I will be referring to and quoting from this remarkable report frequently in the next several pages.) See also Bernstein, *Guns or Butter,* 79; Weisbrot, *Freedom Bound,* 140.

47. Collins to LBJ, n.d., WHCF, Box 25, LBJL.

48. Ibid.

49. Ibid.; Greenstone and Peterson, *Race and Authority,* 160–61.

50. Collins to Shriver, Aug. 23, 1965, and Shriver to Collins, Aug. 23, 1965, WHCF, Box 25, "HU2/ST5 Nov. 22, 1963–Aug. 23, 1965," LBJL.

51. Collins to LBJ, n.d., WHCF, Box 25, "HU2/ST5 Aug. 24, 1965–Sept. 11, 1965," LBJL; Ramsey Clark telegram to Califano, Aug. 30, 1965, WHCF, Box 25, "HU2/ST5 Aug. 24, 1965–Sept. 11, 1965," LBJL; "Collins' Proposal Rejected," *LAS,* Aug. 26, 1965, A1, A8.

52. Collins to LBJ, n.d., WHCF, Box 25, "HU2/ST5 Aug. 24, 1965–Sept. 11, 1965," LBJL.

53. Ibid.

54. Ibid.

55. Ibid.; see also Ramsey Clark telegram to Califano, Aug. 30, 1965, WHCF, Box 25, "HU2/ST5 Aug. 24, 1965–Sept. 11, 1965," LBJL.

56. Califano, *Triumph and Tragedy,* 63–64.

57. Collins to LBJ.

58. Jesse M. Unruh to LBJ, Aug. 26, 1965, White House Central Files, LBJL.

59. "When the Poor are Powerless," *The New Republic,* Sept. 4, 1965, 7.

60. Collins to LBJ, n.d., WHCF, Box 25, LBJL; Greenstone and Peterson, *Race and Authority,* 250; Sonenshein, *Politics in Black and White,* 73.

61. Quote from Erwin Baker, "Angry Mills Quits Poverty War Post," *LAT,* April 19, 1966, I-22; see also Billy Mills to Yorty, April 15, 1966, Boutin Papers, Box 3, "Los Angeles, California," LBJL; and "Mills Exits EYOA, Charges Poverty Program Patronage," *LAS,* April 21, 1966, 1A, 2A.

62. Paul Beck, "Yorty Appoints Brother of Bitter Critic to Poverty Post," *LAT,* April 21, 1966, I-3.

63. Betty Pleasant, "Hawkins' Brothers Clash in EYOA War," *LAS,* April 28, 1966, 7A.

64. Edward Hawkins telegram to Augustus Hawkins, Aug. 6, 1965, Yorty Collection, Box D27, "Hawkins, Edward A.," LACA.

65. "Brother Raps Hawkins for Poverty War Acts," *LAT,* April 30, 1966, I-2; Pleasant, "Hawkins Brothers Clash," *LAS,* April 28, 1966, 1A, 7A.

66. Yorty to City Council, 8/8/67, Yorty Collection, Box D27, "Edward A. Hawkins," LACA.

67. Hawkins to LBJ, Jan. 10, 1966, Boutin Papers, Box 3, "Los Angeles, California," LBJL.

68. Edgar May to Shriver, Feb. 7, 1966, WHCF Confidential Files, Box 98, "WE9 Poverty Program (Great Society) (1964–1966)" LBJL.

69. Yete to Boutin and Shriver, Jan. 1, 1966; and Sam Proctor to Boutin, Mar. 18, 1966, Boutin Papers, Box 3, "Los Angeles, California," LBJL.

Chapter 3

1. NAPP Progress Report, Aug. 1, 1965, NAPP Records, Box 3, USC; "NAPP Now: An Explanation of the Neighborhood Adult Participation Project," NAPP Records, Box 1, USC.

2. NAPP Progress Report, Aug. 1, 1965, NAPP Records, Box 3, USC; NAPP Annual Report, 1966, LAAFSNC Records, Box 2, USC; ABT Associates, Inc., "A Neighborhood Program Unit Report on the Neighborhood Adult Participation Project," January 1970, Roybal Papers, Box 190, CSLA; "NAPP Now: An Explanation of the Neighborhood Adult Participation Project," NAPP Records, Box 1, USC; Jack Jones, "Opal Jones Mellows as Poverty Project Grows," *Los Angeles Times*, March 30, 1967; "NAPP Fights Poverty With Total Grass-Roots Approach," *LAS*, June 10, 1965, 10A; "Neglect of Mexican-American Group in Poverty War Charged," *LAT*, Aug. 1, 1966, I-3.

3. Yette to Boutin and Shriver, Jan. 14, 1966, Boutin Papers, Box 3, "Los Angeles, California," LBJL.

4. Boutin to Daniel Luevano, Mar. 3, 1966; L. E. Williams to Theodore Berry, Apr. 1, 1966; and Boutin to Califano, Apr. 6, 1966, Boutin Papers, Box 3, "Los Angeles, California"; Daniel M. Luevano to Shriver, Mar. 21, 1966, Boutin Papers, Box 21, "RS-Western Region," all LBJL.

5. Opal Jones to EYOA (Attention: Joe Maldonado), April 1, 1966, NAPP Records, Box 2, USC; Boutin to Califano, Apr. 6, 1966, Boutin Papers, Box 3, "Los Angeles, California," LBJL; Betty Pleasant, "Opal Jones Views Fight: Hearing on Dismissal Set Wednesday," *LAS*, April 7, 1966, A1, D2; Marshall, *Politics of Participation in Poverty*, 19.

6. Boutin to Califano, Apr. 6, 1966, Boutin Papers, Box 3, "Los Angeles, California," LBJL; Roy Rogers, "Crowd Holds Rally to Protest Firing of Poverty Aide," *LAT*, April 6, 1966; Pleasant, "Opal Jones Views Fight," *LAS*, April 17, 1966, A1, D2.

7. Boutin to Califano, Apr. 6, 1966, Boutin Papers, Box 3, "Los Angeles, California," LBJL.

8. Luevano to various officials, May 2, 1966, Boutin Papers, Box 3, "Los Angeles, California," LBJL; "Rights Official Hails Poverty War Shake-Up," *LAT*, Apr. 9, 1966, II-10; Jack Jones, "Clarified Rules Sought in Poverty War Here," *LAT*, 5/3/66, I-16; Betty Pleasant, "Yorty Hits Hawkins, Upholds Maldonado," *LAS*, April 14, 1966, A1.

9. "Rights Official Hails Poverty War Shake-Up," *LAT*, Apr. 9, 1966, II-10.

10. "The OEO Decision: Making for Action," editorial, *LAS*, April 14, 1966, 6A.

11. Erwin Baker, "Angry Mills Quits Poverty War Post," *LAT*, April 19, 1966, I-3, 22; Betty Pleasant, "Legal Fight Seen in Poverty War," *LAS*, April 14, 1966, 1A, 2A.

12. Betty Pleasant, "Hawkins Brothers Clash in EYOA War," *LAS*, Apr. 28, 1966, 7A.

13. Yorty to LBJ, Apr. 11, 1966, Boutin Papers, Box 3, "Los Angeles, California," LBJL.

14. Yorty to LBJ, Apr. 25, 1966, WHCF, Box 9 "LG/Los Angeles," LBJL.

15. Betty Pleasant, "Yorty Hits Hawkins, Upholds Maldonado," *LAS*, Apr. 14, 1966, A1, A2.

16. Ibid.

17. Shriver to Yorty, telegram, Apr. 23, 1966, Yorty Collection, Box D25, "Office of Economic Opportunity," LACA; Greenstone and Peterson, *Race and Authority*, 33; Jack Jones, "Ousted Poverty Aide Rehired in Stormy Session," *LAT*, Apr. 26, 1966, I-1.

18. "EYOA Reinstates Mrs. Opal Jones," *LAS*, Apr. 28, 1966, 1A; Jack Jones, "Ousted Poverty Aide Rehired in Stormy Session," *LAT*, Apr. 26, 1966, I-1; "Neglect of Mexican-American Group in Poverty War Charged," *LAT*, Aug. 1, 1966, I-3; "EYOA Releases Control of Opal Jones' NAPP," *LAT*, Aug. 4, 1966, 4A; Greenstone and Peterson, *Race and Authority*, 33.

19. Opal Jones, "The Mexican Americans in NAPP," n.d., NAPP Records, Box 3, USC.

20. Opal Jones to Gabriel Yánez, September 8, 1966, NAPP Records, Box 3, USC; "Opal Jones Fires Aide for 'Ineffectiveness,'" *LAS*, Sept. 6, 1966, A1, A3; Greenstone and Peterson, *Race and Authority*, 211–12.

21. Art Berman, "Latin-American Quits Antipoverty Job in a Row," *LAT*, Sept. 16, 1966, I-32.

22. Opal Jones to Isobel C. Clark, September 26, 1966, and Opal Jones to Gabriel Yánez, June 10, 1966, both NAPP Records, Box 3, USC; Art Berman, "Latin-AmericanQuits Antipoverty Job in a Row," *LAT*, Sept. 16, 1966, I-32.

23. Irene Tovar's career later led her to a job with the Los Angeles County Civil Service Commission in the early 1970s and as Special Assistant to California Governor Jerry Brown in the late 1970s and early 1980s. Jack Jones, "Irate Mexican-American Units Demand Poverty War Equality," *LAT*, Sept. 25, 1966, I-20; Oropeza, *¡Raza Sí! ¡Guerra No!*, 156–57; Greenstone and Peterson, *Race and Authority*, 211–12.

24. Luevano to Roybal, Aug. 12, 1966, and NAPP Project Committee minutes, Oct. 19, 1966, both NAPP Records, Box 3, USC; NAPP Project Committee minutes, Dec. 7, 1966, EYOA Records, Box 1, USC; Los Angeles Area Federation of Settlements and Neighborhood Centers, Executive Director's Report, September–Octo-

ber 1966, LAAFSNC Records, Box 2, USC; LAAFSNC Board of Directors Meeting Minutes, Oct. 20, 1966 and Nov. 17, 1966, LAAFSNC Records, Box 2, USC.

25. LAAFSNC Board of Directors Meeting Minutes, Jan. 19, 1967, May 18, 1967, and June 15, 1967, all LAAFSNC Records, Box 1, USC; NAPP Quarterly Report, April–June 1967, NAPP Records, Box 1, USC.

26. Roybal to Paul Ramirez, Oct. 5, 1966, Roybal Papers, Box 193, Folder 25—"Teen Posts," CSLA.

27. Roybal to Sarah Taylor, Oct. 20, 1967, and Jones to Roybal Aug. 21, 1968, both Roybal Papers, Box 190, CSLA. For more on the labor and Mexican American civil rights activist Bert Corona, see Mario T. Garcia, *Memories of Chicano History.*

28. "NAPP Now: An Explanation of the Neighborhood Adult Participation Project," NAPP Records, Box 1; ABT Associates, Inc., "Neighborhood Action Site Report: A Neighborhood Program Unit Report on the NAPP, Inc.," NAPP Records, Box 2; Betty Pleasant, "The Mobility of NAPP Aides: A Research Study, September 1968," NAPP Records, Box 4, all USC.

29. Shriver to Boutin, May 4, 1966; and unidentified person to Shriver, n.d., Boutin Papers, Box 3, "Los Angeles, California." Luevano's prominent position within the Johnson administration was in part due his Mexican American heritage, which Johnson and Governor Brown both thought would be helpful in garnering votes in 1964. He had previously served as Brown's chief deputy director of finance and as an assistant secretary of the army. LBJ chose him to be the regional director of OEO the day following the Watts revolt. See Recording of Telephone conversation between LBJ and Brown, February 14, 1964, 11:30 A.M., Citation #2076, Recordings of Telephone Conversations—White House Series, LBJL; and Luevano, Oral History Interview by Carlos Vasquez, UCLA Oral History Program for the California State Archives State Government Oral History Program, 1988.

30. Shriver to Yorty, May 12, 1966; and Clifford Alexander to Fred Vinson, May 5, 1966, WHCF, "LG/Los Angeles" Box 9, LBJL.

31. Shriver to Yorty, May 12, 1966, Yorty Collection, Box D25, "Office of Economic Opportunity," LACA.

32. "Four Agencies Set Up to Direct Poverty War," *LAT,* Aug. 12, 1966, II-1.

33. OEO Press Release, Dec. 17, 1968, Roybal Papers, Box 191, CSLA; Jack Jones, "Poverty Official Probes East L.A. Charges," *LAT,* Sept. 1, 1968, II-1; Jack Jones, "Run Programs Again, Poverty Agency Urged," *LAT,* Feb. 18, 1969, II-5; Ray Zeman, "EYOA Picked to Run Poverty Program in East L.A., 5 Cities," *LAT,* Mar. 12, 1969, II-1.

34. Roybal to EYOA Board of Directors, Oct. 8, 1971, and Roybal to Phil Sanchez, Oct. 8, 1971, both Roybal Papers, Box 192, CSLA; EYOA Board Minutes, June 1, 1969, Hawkins Papers, Box 94, UCLA; Acuña, *A Community under Siege,* 185, 219–20; Robert Kistler, "Chaos Follows Conference on 'Harmony' in EYOA Program," *LAT,* Apr. 29, 1972, II-1, 8; Jack Jones, "$7.9 Million Poverty Package Ok'd; Row Delays Finance Plan," *LAT,* Oct. 15, 1969, II-1, 8.

35. Esteban Torres and Richard Martinez, Congress of Mexican-American Unity to OEO, January 15, 1971; David Lizarraga, Chicano Caucus to OEO, January 11, 1971; and David Lizarraga to Congressman Carl Perkins, February 16, 1971, all Roybal Papers, Box 191, CSLA.

36. Knox to Hawkins, Nov. 17, 1971; Knox to Lorenzo Traylor, Mar. 17, 1972; and Knox to Virna Canson, Sept. 21, 1972; all Hawkins Papers, Box 96, UCLA.

37. Celeste Durant, "EYOA Fund Cut Aimed at Blacks, Chief Says," *LAT,* Aug. 28, 1972, I-3; Jack Jones, "EYOA 'Death-Warrant' Decision Stated Today," *LAT,* Aug. 31, 1972, II-1, 8.

38. Chicano Coalition Press Release, Mar. 8, 1974; Chicano Coalition Meeting Minutes, May 30, 1974; John Serrano, Chair of Chicano Coalition to Supervisor Baxter Ward, June 7, 1974; and Chicano Coalition Press Release, Oct. 29, 1974; all Roybal Papers, Box 37, CSLA; and "County Poverty Unit Settles Suit Charging Bias," *LAT,* June 2, 1975, I-30.

39. "City Rejects Poverty Agency's Fund Request," *LAT,* Aug. 15, 1975, II-5; Ray Zeman, "Solve Crisis or Fire Official, Agency Told," *LAT,* Dec. 24, 1975, II-1; Bruce Keppel, "Supervisors Vote to Terminate Poverty Agency," *LAT,* June 28, 1978, I-3, 32; Bruce Keppel, "Poverty Agency Workers Face job Loss," *LAT,* Dec. 9, 1978, I-31.

Chapter 4

1. Testimony of Paul Schrade, Oct. 6, 1967, Kerner Commission Transcripts, Box 4, LBJL.

2. "Staff Report of Actions Taken to Implement Recommendations of Governor's Commission," Aug. 18, 1967, Ramsey Clark Papers, Box 76, "Watts August 1965," LBJL; *Watts Labor Community Action Committee, 1967 Report,* 1, UCLA; "Outsiders Running War on Poverty," *LAS,* May 27, 1965, A11; Myrna Oliver, "Watts Activist Ted Watkins, Sr. Dies at 71," *LAT,* November 11, 1993, B-1, 4.

3. Quoted in Harry Bernstein, *Guns or Butter,* "Ted Watkins: He Gets Things Accomplished," *LAT,* Mar. 23, 1975, II-10.

4. *Watts Labor Community Action Committee, 1967 Report*; Paul Bullock, "On Organizing the Poor: Problems of Morality and Tactics," *Dissent* 15, no. 1 (Jan.–Feb. 1968); "Staff Report of Actions Taken," Aug. 18, 1967, Ramsey Clark Papers, Box 76, "Watts August 1965," LBJL; Horne, *Fire This Time,* 276–77; "Watts Union Workers Form Action Committee," *LAS,* Aug. 26, 1965, 4A; "Watts Group Sets Meeting," *LAS,* Oct. 21, 1965, 2A; Jack Jones, "Watts Job Project Instilling Initiative in School Dropouts," *LAT,* Apr. 17, 1967, II-1.

5. First quote is in letter from Reuther to President Johnson, June 26, 1964, White House Central Files, WE-9, LBJL. Second quote is from Testimony of Paul Schrade, Oct. 6, 1967, Kerner Commission Transcripts, Box 4, LBJL. On the UAW's involvement in the War on Poverty and its concomitant representation of a new constituency, low-wage disenfranchised workers, see Coleman, "Labor Power

and Social Equality," 687–705. See also Horne, *Fire This Time*, 250–51; Boyle, *The UAW and the Heyday*; and Lichtenstein, *The Most Dangerous Man in Detroit*.

6. See letter from Reuther to Johnson, June 26, 1964, WHCF, WE-9, LBJL.

7. Boyle, *The UAW and the Heyday*, 188.

8. Quote is from ibid., 213–14. See also Unger, *The Best of Intentions*, 168–69.

9. TELACU is the focus of chapter 4. First quote is from handwritten note from LBJ to Marvin Watson on memo from Watson to LBJ, Feb. 27, 1968, WHCF, WE9, Box 31, LBJL. Second quote is Acuña, *A Community under Siege*, 185–86. For information on Reuther and UAW's involvement in the War on Poverty, see Boyle, *The UAW and the Heyday*, 223–24, and Lichtenstein, *Most Dangerous Man in Detroit*, 39, 389–90.

10. Testimony of Paul Schrade, Oct. 6, 1967, Kerner Commission Transcripts, Box 4, LBJL.

11. Quoted in "Watts Union Workers Form Action Committee," *LAS*, Aug. 26, 1965, 4A.

12. UAW Report quoted in John R. Chávez, *Eastside Landmark*, 29.

13. "Staff Report of Actions Taken," Aug. 18, 1967, Ramsey Clark Papers, Box 76, "Watts August 1965," LBJL; Myrna Oliver, "Watts Activist Ted Watkins, Sr. Dies at 71," *LAT*, November 11, 1993, B-1, 4; "Labor Group Urges Action Programs," *LAS*, Sept. 9, 1965, 8A.

14. "The Watts Labor Community Action Committee," brochure, in "Watts 1960s" folder, SCL; Malaika Brown, "WLCAC's Ted Watkins Leaves Valuable Living Legacy," *LAS*, Nov. 11, 1993, A3.

15. "The Watts Labor Community Action Committee," brochure, in "Watts 1960s" folder, SCL; "Ted Watkins Resolution," in folder 13, "Ted Watkins," Mervyn Dymally Papers, Box 141, CSLA; Malaika Brown, "WLCAC's Ted Watkins Leaves Valuable Living Legacy," *LAS*, Nov. 11, 1993, A3.

16. "Watts Labor Action Committee Gets Praise, $260,806 Grant from OEO," *LAS*, July 13, 1967, A1; Harry Bernstein, "Labor-Backed Group in Watts Given $260,806," *LAT*, July 11, 1967, II-1, 3; Boyle, 214.

17. Marshall Lowe, "WLCAC Gets $2 Million For New Low Cost Homes," *LAS*, Mar. 4, 1971, A1, 12.

18. First quote is from Ford Foundation, "Community Development Corporations: A Strategy for Depressed Urban and Rural Areas: A Ford Foundation Policy Paper," May 1973, TELACU Records, Box 5, CSLA. Second quote is from The Urban Institute, "Evaluating Community Development Corporations—A Summary Report," March 1976, TELACU Records, Box 5, CSLA. Third quote is from "Hispanic American Coalition for Economic Revitalization (HACER): Final Report 1980," TELACU Records, Box 4, CSLA.

19. Los Angeles City Council File #104020, Supplement 11, LACA; Myrna Oliver, "Watts Activist Ted Watkins, Sr. Dies at 71," *LAT*, November 11, 1993, B-1, 4; "The Watts Labor Community Action Committee," brochure, in "Watts 1960s"

folder, SCL; Harry Bernstein, "Ted Watkins: He Gets Things Accomplished," *LAT,* Mar. 23, 1975, II-10; WLCAC advertisement, *LAS,* Nov. 1, 1971, A11.

20. Harry Bernstein, "Labor-Backed Group in Watts Given $260,806," *LAT,* July 11, 1967, II-1, 3; "Watts Action Group Gets $320,000 Manpower Funds," *LAT,* July 21, 1966, 4A.

21. The Saugus Center remained in operation until 1973, when it was eliminated as a result of Department of Labor funding cuts and administrative problems. "Staff Report of Actions Taken," Aug. 18, 1967, Ramsey Clark Papers, Box 76, "Watts August 1965" LBJL; "The Watts Labor Community Action Committee," brochure, in "Watts 1960s" folder, SCL; Harry Bernstein, "Many Help to Put Across Watts-Army Camp Plan," *LAT,* Aug. 16, 1967, II-6; Joe Bingham, "Watts Labor Leader Turns U.S. Upside Down for Kids," *LAS,* Aug. 17, 1967, 1A; Bill Graham to the President, June 16, 1967, Califano Files, Box 58, "Watts," LBJL; Philip Lawlor to Ted Watkins, Jan. 18, 1973, Hawkins Papers, UCLA.

22. Testimony of Paul Schrade, Oct. 6, 1967, Kerner Commission Transcripts, Box 4, LBJL; Jack Jones, "Watts Job Effort Pays Dividends," *LAT,* Jan. 29, 1968, II-1; "McCone Heads Watts Hospital Unit," *LAHE,* Apr. 19, 1967; Bauman, "From Tuberculosis Sanatorium to Medical Center," 210.

23. Janet Clayton, "Watts' Buying Power Tied to 1st and 15th," *LAT,* Aug. 21, 1980.

24. See Unger, *The Best of Intentions.*

25. "The Watts Labor Community Action Committee," brochure, in folder "Watts 1960s," SCL.

26. "Watts Labor Community Action Committee, Community Conservation Corps Final Report, July 1967," 5–6; Los Angeles City Council Resolution, November 22, 1966, Los Angeles City Council File #129596-1; and Los Angeles City Council Resolution, February 21, 1968, Los Angeles City Council File #138000, all LACA; WLCAC 1967 Report.

27. WLCAC 1967 Report, 8–9, 36–39; California Department of Industrial Relations, Division of Labor Statistics and Research, *Negroes and Mexican Americans in South and East Los Angeles.*

28. WLCAC 1967 Report; "Watts Labor Community Action Committee, Community Conservation Corps Final Report, July 1967," 5–6, UCLA; Robert Perrin to Seymour Brandwein, Dept. of Labor, Nov. 1, 1966, WHCF; "Staff Report of Actions Taken," Aug. 18, 1967, Ramsey Clark Papers, Box 76, "Watts August 1965," LBJL; Jack Jones, "Watts Job Project Instilling Initiative in School Dropouts," *LAT,* Aug. 17, 1967, II-1.

29. "Watts Labor Community Action Committee, 1967 Report." UCLA.

30. Stanley Sanders quote is from Chapman, *Black Voices,* 352. See also Gordon, "Fortifying Community," 77–79 (quote from p. 79); Horne, *Fire This Time,* 276–78; Jack Jones, "Watts Job Effort Pays Dividends," *LAT,* Jan. 29, 1968, II-1, 2; Jack Jones, "The Programs: At Least Somebody Cared," *LAT,* Mar. 23, 1975, II-4.

31. For information on the Black Power movement, especially its cultural influence, see Van DeBurg, *New Day in Babylon.*

32. Tyler, "Rise and Decline," 63–66; Glasgow, "Sons of Watts Improvement Association," 4–5; "LAAFSNC Annual Report 1966," LAAFSNC Records, Box 1, USC.

33. "Poverty Chief to Lead Watts Parade," *LAS,* Aug. 11, 1966, 1A.

34. Tyler, "Rise and Decline," 67–68. For more on black power and its varieties, see Joseph, *Waiting 'Til the Midnight Hour,* and Joseph, *The Black Power Movement.*

35. Tyler, "Rise and Decline," 62, 66–74; quote is from 66. See also "Watts Summer Festival: Pride and Progress," 1967 program, Watts Collection, USC.

36. Testimony of Paul Schrade, Oct. 6, 1967, Kerner Commission Transcripts, Box 4, LBJL.

37. Ibid.; Harry Bernstein, "Ted Watkins: He Gets Things Accomplished," *LAT,* Mar, 23, 1975, II-2, 10.

38. Los Angeles City Council Resolution, February 21, 1968, Los Angeles City Council File #138000, LACA.

39. Bob Strunk of the Ford Foundation, quoted in Harry Bernstein, "Ted Watkins: He Gets Things Accomplished," *LAT,* Mar. 23, 1975, II-2.

40. Bettina Boxall, "Jazz-Filled Memorial to Watts Activist," *LAT,* November 14, 1993, A-1.

41. Ibid., A-34.

42. For information on national and international market forces that have negatively impacted America's inner cities, see Nightingale, "The Global Inner City," 217–58; Thomas J. Sugrue, "The Structures of Urban Poverty: The Reorganization of Space and Work in Three Periods of American History," 85–117; Oliver, Johnson, and Farrell, "Anatomy of a Rebellion," 117–41; and Wilson, *When Work Disappears.*

43. Marita Hernandez and Austin Scott, "New Strains Emerge as Watts Evolves," *LAT,* Aug. 24, 1980; Pitt and Pitt, *Los Angeles A to Z,* 5, 537; Navarro, "The Latinoization of Los Angeles," 170–71.

Chapter 5

1. Sánchez, *Becoming Mexican American*; Bureau of the Census, *U.S. Census of the Population, 1950*; Bureau of the Census, *U.S. Census of Population, 1960.*

2. TELACU Community Research Group, "Greater East Los Angeles Cultural Heritage Survey," January 1979, TELACU Records, Box 4, CSLA.

3. TELACU, "Preferences & Issues Survey Sub-Program, Unincorporated East Los Angeles Social and Community Environmental Assessment Program, Volume II," 1976; TELACU, "The East Los Angeles Proposed Community Plan: The East Los Angeles Environmental Assessment Program," both TELACU Records, Box 1, CSLA; State of California, *Negroes and Mexican Americans in South and East Los Angeles,* 23–24.

4. Quote is from John A. Buggs to Alex Garcia, September 10, 1963, Roybal

Papers, Box 19, Folder 24—"Discrimination, Human Relations," CSLA. See also Banfield, *Big City Politics,* 87–90; Horne, *Fire This Time,* 102, 260–61; Gómez-Quiñones, *Chicano Politics,* 95; Marquez, *LULAC,* 7; Laslett, "Historical Perspectives," 56, 67; Sides, "Rethinking Black Migration," 204–208; Leonard, *The Battle for Los Angeles,* 311, 326–27; Henry, "Black-Chicano Coalitions," 222–32; and Martinez and Longeaux y Vasquez, *Viva La Raza!*

5. Acuña, *A Community under Siege,* 124, 132; Sonenshein, *Politics in Black and White,* 85.

6. Acuña, *A Community under Siege,* 131, 175–76.

7. Andy Hilton to Shriver, Oct. 14, 1965, Boutin Papers, Box 3, "FA California" LBJL. Hernandez is quoted in Pycior, *LBJ and Mexican Americans,* 163. See also Acuña, *A Community under Siege,* 132–33.

8. Quoted in Jack Jones, "Irate Mexican-American Units Demand Poverty War Equality," *LAT,* Sept. 25, 1966, A3. See also Pycior, *LBJ and Mexican Americans,* 153–63; and Henry, *Black-Chicano Coalitions,* 222–32.

9. Scholars have debated the origins of the word "Chicano," but it came into use by young Mexican Americans as a way to define themselves, connect themselves to their historical and cultural past, and break from previous attempts at assimilation to demand economic, cultural, and political change. See Mariscal, *Brown-Eyed Children*; Ernesto Chávez, *¡Mi Raza Primero!,* 43–47; and López, *Racism on Trial,* 178–82. Chicanas were actively involved in the YCCA and the Brown Berets. See Espinoza, "'Revolutionary Sisters,'" 17–58.

10. Quote is from Escobar, "The Dialectics of Repression," 1483. See also Oropeza, *¡Raza Sí! ¡Guerra No!,* esp. chap. 5; Mariscal, *Aztlán and Viet Nam*; Gonzales, *Mexicanos,* 208–15; and Martinez interview, 64–66.

11. The Chicana Service Action Center is the focus of chapter 5. See, Pycior, *LBJ and Mexican Americans,* 158–61, 208; Pitt and Pitt, *Los Angeles A to Z,* 130; Vicki L. Ruiz, *From Out of the Shadows,* 114. This study does not address community organizations, such as the United Neighborhoods Organization (UNO), that were not directly connected to the framework or programs of the War on Poverty. The UNO was a joint venture of Catolicos Por La Raza (a group formed out of the Chicano movement) and the Catholic Church in East Los Angeles. See Ortiz, "Chicano Urban Politics," 564–77.

12. John R. Chávez, *Eastside Landmark,* 2–3, 33–39; quote is from 39. See also Marín, *Social Protest,* 173–74; "O'Loane Marks a Decade of Service with TELACU," *TELACU Today* 1, no. 6 (January 1978); "President Carter Selects TELACU's Esteban Torres as Special Assistant," *TELACU Today* 3, no. 2 (October 1979).

13. Torres, quoted in John R. Chávez, *Eastside Landmark,* 11.

14. Solis quote is from "Board Chair George Solis Works Behind the Scenes to Make TELACU Work," *TELACU Today* 3, no. 3 (January–February 1980). O'Loane quote is from "O'Loane Marks a Decade."

15. "The East Los Angeles Community Union."

16. Marín, *Social Protest,* 174–75; John R. Chávez, *Eastside Landmark,* 35–37, 59–64; "O'Loane Marks a Decade."

17. "Social Services" folder, TELACU Records, Box 4; "TELACU Family Health Center Opens in Highland Park," *TELACU Today* 4, no. 1 (January–February 1981), TELACU Records, Box 1, CSLA.

18. John R. Chávez, *Eastside Landmark,* 95–106, 168–93; Marín, *Social Protest,* 187–95.

19. TELACU Quarterly Report to Community Services Administration, Office of Economic Opportunity, December 1975; and "ELABDC: A Division of TELACU," pamphlet, both TELACU Records, Box 4, CSLA. TELACU, "Nueva Maravilla Affirmative Action Program," TELACU Records, Box 5, CSLA. John A. Echeveste, "TELACU: Pioneers in Economic Development," *Opportunity II* (Fall 1978): 16.

20. TELACU, "Barrio Housing Plan: TELACU's Development Strategy and Immediate Direction," June 1971, TELACU Records, Box 2, CSLA.

21. Center for Community Economic Development, "TELACU."

22. Quote about murals is from Rojas, "Cultural Landscape," 180. See also "The East Los Angeles Community Union"; Art Seidenbaum, "East L.A. Accents the Positive," *LAT,* June 24, 1977, IV-1, 12; "TELACU Industrial Park to Spark a New Economic Revival in East LA," *TELACU Today* 1, no. 5 (November 1977), TELACU Records, Box 1, CSLA; "TELACU Industrial Park: From Blueprints to Reality in 365 Days," *TELACU Today* 2, no. 3 (September–October 1978), TELACU Records, Box 1, CSLA.

23. Abel Salas, "Snapshots from the Center of the Universe: Eastside Masterpiece—Tamayo Restaurant Still Honors Art and Eating," *Los Angeles Times Magazine,* July 6, 2003, 1, 6; John R. Chávez, *Eastside Landmark,* 231–34.

24. TELACU, "Barrio Housing Plan: TELACU's Development Strategy and Immediate Direction," June 1971, TELACU Records, Box 2, CSLA.

25. Lizarraga quotes are from John A. Echeveste, "TELACU: Pioneers in Economic Development," *Opportunity II* (Fall 1978), 16, TELACU Records, Box 1, CSLA. See also George Ramos, "Author Takes Upbeat View of East L.A. Institution," *LAT,* April 27, 1999.

26. Center for Community Economic Development, "TELACU"; John R. Chávez, *Eastside Landmark,* 110–11.

27. TELACU, "Nueva Maravilla Affirmative Action program"; TELACU, "Maravilla Neighborhood Development Program Citizen Participation and Community Involvement," TELACU Records, Box 5, CSLA; John R. Chávez, *Eastside Landmark,* 82–83.

28. Echeveste, "TELACU," 16; TELACU, "Nueva Maravilla Affirmative Action Program"; TELACU, "Maravilla Neighborhood Development Program Citizen Participation and Community Involvement," TELACU Records, Box 5, CSLA; Center for Community Economic Development, "TELACU: Community Development for the Future," TELACU Records, Box 1, CSLA.

29. TELACU, "Community Research Group," TELACU Records, Box 4, CSLA; TELACU, "Whittier Boulevard Commercial Revitalization Project: Final Environmental Impact Report," June 1980, TELACU Records, Box 2, CSLA; and John R. Chávez, *Eastside Landmark*, 224–25.

30. Ramos, "Author Takes Upbeat View."

31. Hugo Martin, "A Savvy Housing Group Expands: The East Los Angeles Community Union, Known for Cultivating Latino Leaders, Builds in the Inland Empire," *LAT*, Dec. 27, 2004.

32. Echeveste, "TELACU," 18.

33. Ibid.; Molina interview, 329–31; Martin, "A Savvy Housing Group Expands."

34. Martinez interview, 57–59.

35. Quoted in Ramos, "Author Takes Upbeat View."

36. The board-member quote is from Marín, *Social Protest*, 179. The Lizarraga quote is from "The East Los Angeles Community Union."

37. Quote is from UAW Report, quoted in John R. Chávez, *Eastside Landmark*, 29.

38. Quote is from "TELACU Industries Assisting Two Businesses," *TELACU Today* 2, no. 1 (May–June 1978), TELACU Records, Box 5, CSLA. See also HACER Report; Luis Lopez, TELACU Project Director, to Mildred Glazer, Department of Commerce, May 30, 1980, TELACU Records, Box 4, CSLA; John R. Chávez, *Eastside Landmark*, 259–64.

39. Report of the Twentieth Century Fund Task Force on Community Development Corporation, *CDCs: New Hope for the Inner City*, 42; Orleck, *Storming Caesar's Palace*, 259.

40. Quote is from *CDCs: New Hope for the Inner City*, 42. Orleck makes this important point about gender disparities in CDC funding. See Orleck, *Storming Caesar's Palace*, 259–60.

41. Orleck, *Storming Caesar's Palace*, 268–70.

42. John R. Chávez, *Eastside Landmark*, 255; Hispanic Business.com, www.hispanicbusiness.com/research/500/view.

43. Greater Los Angeles Community Action Agency, "Council 10 Needs Statement and Goals—Poverty Planning Area 10—East Los Angeles," TELACU Records, Box 5, CSLA.

44. Art Seidenbaum, "East L.A. Accents the Positive," *LAT*, June 24, 1977, part 4, 1, 12.

45. John R. Chávez, *Eastside Landmark*, 12–13.

46. For a similar multiracial perspective on the War on Poverty in another community in the West, see the excellent article by William Clayson, "The Barrios and the Ghettos," 158–84.

Chapter 6

1. "History of Comisión Femenil de Los Angeles, Feb. 1983," Part I, Collection 30, Box 1, Folder 6, CFLA-UCLA; Nieto Gomez, "Chicana Service Action Center," 148–49; "Preliminary Ideas for Women's Workshop," Comisión Femenil Mexicana Nacional Archives Collection, Series V, CSAC, CFMN-CEMA, Box 38, Folder 3; Nava interview by Michelle Moravec.

2. "Resolution Establishing Comisión Femenil Mexicana Nacional," CFMN-CEMA, Box 1, Folder 7.

3. Nava interview by Michelle Moravec, interview 1b, segment 1 (0:00–3:52), Segkey: cfs619.

4. Flores interview.

5. Isasi-Diaz, Olazagasti-Segovia et al., "Roundtable Discussion: Mujeristas," 105–28. First quote is from Isasi-Diaz; additional quotes are from Olazagasti-Segovia.

6. "History of Comisión Femenil de Los Angeles," CFLA-UCLA.

7. Alma M. Garcia, "Introduction," 1–16.

8. Flores, "Comisión Femenil Mexicana."

9. Flores interview.

10. Dr. Bill Flores, May 2, 1996, "Francisca Flores," http:///latino.sscnet.ucla.edu/research/francisca.html; Bill Gutierrez to Mrs. Frances Flores, April 18, 1963, CFMN-CEMA, Box 38, Folder 1; "Francisca Flores Vitae," CFMN-CEMA, Box 40, Folder 1.

11. Flores to Philip Ortega, n.d. (1968), CFMN-CEMA, Box 41, Folder 7.

12. *Carta Editorial,* July 3, 1963, 7; *Carta Editorial,* November 23, 1965, 3; Oropeza, *¡Raza Si! ¡Guerra No!,* 65–66.

13. Graciela Olivarez to Francisca Flores, November 26, 1963, CFMN-CEMA, Box 38, Folder 1.

14. Olivarez to Flores, December 17, 1963, CFMN-CEMA, Box 38, Folder 1.

15. Father Theodore Hesburgh, President of the University of Notre Dame, 1952–87, and member of the U.S. Commission on Civil Rights, 1957–72 (he served as chair from 1969 to 1972).

16. Olivarez to Flores, July 28, 1964, CFMN-CEMA, Box 38, Folder 1.

17. Marina Mireles, "Grievances of East L.A. Mexican Americans Aired," *LAHE,* June 10, 1967, CFMN-CEMA, Box 38, Folder 2.

18. Olivarez to Flores, October 6, 1964, CFMN-CEMA, Box 41, Folder 3. VISTA (Volunteers in Service to America) was one of the War on Poverty programs created by the Economic Opportunity Act of 1964.

19. Olivarez to Flores, January 6, 1965, CFMN-CEMA, Box 41, Folder 4.

20. "Francisca Flores Vitae," Box 40, Folder 1; Barrying Morrison to Flores, December 10, 1965, Box 41, Folder 5; Kenneth Washington to Flores, December 12, 1966, Box 41, Folder 5; Julia T. Cellini to Flores, April 24, 1967; Charlotte Lewis

to Flores, May 5, 1967; William Crook to Flores, May 19, 1967, latter three all Box 41, Folder 6, all CFMN-CEMA.

21. "History of Comisión Femenil De Los Angeles," CFLA-UCLA; Nava interview by Moravec; Minutes of CSAC Board of Directors Meeting, July 7, 1972, CFMN-CEMA, Box 38, Folder 5. While CSAC's first year was funded by the Department of Labor through the Manpower Development and Training Act (MDTA), in 1973 its contract was extended through the Economic Opportunity Act. On the Nixon administration's attacks on OEO and the shifting of programs to the Department of Labor, see Bauman, "Race, Class and Political Power,"109–14.

22. CSAC Original Proposal, CFMN-CEMA, Box 38, Folder 6.

23. Nieto Gomez, "Chicanas in the Labor Force"; handwritten notes for CSAC Board Agenda, August 16, 1973, CFMN-CEMA, Box 38, Folder 5.

24. Cloward and Ohlin, *Delinquency and Opportunity.*

25. "Women's Job Training Program" brochure, CFMN-CEMA, Box 43, Folder 24; Nieto Gomez, "Chicana Service Action Center," 148–49.

26. CSAC Newsletters, November 1973 and May 1977, Box 2, Folder—"Chicana Service Action Center," CFLA-UCLA.

27. Francisca Flores, "General Administrative History of CSAC," n.d., CFMN-CEMA, Box 43, Folder 21.

28. "CSAC Summary Report for November 1973" and "CSAC Summary Report for December 1974," CFMN-CEMA, Box 38, Folder 8; "CSAC News," Newsletter #9, January 1, 1974, CFMN-CEMA, Box 38, Folder 10.

29. CSAC Report, August 1973–May 1974; CFMN-CEMA, Box 39, Folder 3; General Administrative History of CSAC, CFMN-CEMA, Box 43, Folder 21.

30. CSAC Newsletter, July 1975, Box 2, Folder—"Chicana Service Action Center," CFLA-UCLA.

31. Kathleen Hendrix, "Action Center Helps Women Set New Goals," *LAT,* October 22, 1975.

32. Ibid.

33. CSAC Women's Managerial Manpower Training Program and Women's Pre-Apprenticeship Program brochures, CFMN-CEMA, Box 43, Folder 24.

34. CSAC Oral Presentation at Los Angeles County CETA Appeals Committee, CFMN-CEMA, Box 39, Folder 1; CSAC Executive Board Meeting Minutes, November 14, 1974, Box 39, Folder 2.

35. Mark Sanders, Executive Secretary of California Manpower Services Council to Flores, October 21, 1974, CFMN-CEMA, Box 39, Folder 3; Steven M. Porter, Assistant Director Manpower and Training Division of City of Los Angeles, December 23, 1974, CFMN-CEMA, Box 39, Folder 4; Flores to CFMN Members, December 2, 1974, CFMN-CEMA, Box 70, Folder 5.

36. Orleck, *Storming Caesar's Palace,* 224, 240, 274; Franklin and Ripley, *C.E.T.A.: Politics and Policy, 1973–1982.*

37. CSAC News Release, 1976, CFMN-CEMA, Box 43, Folder 1.

38. Nava interview with Moravec, Interview 1b, Segment 4 (11:14–16:37) Segkey: cfs622; "History of Comisión Femenil de Los Angeles," CSAC Newsletter, December 1973; "Centro de Niños History," n.d., CFMN-CEMA, Box 49, Folder 2.

39. Sandra Serrano Sewell to Francisca Flores, April 6, 1976, CFMN-CEMA, Box 39, Folder 7; "Centro de Niños History," n.d., CFMN-CEMA, Box 49, Folder 2; "Centro de Niños Proposal and Abstract," 1973, CFMN-CEMA, Box 49, Folder 3.

40. CFLA-UCLA, Part II, Box 1, Collection 31; "Shelter for Battered Women—Bilingual" brochure, CFMN-CEMA, Box 39, Folder 7; "CSAC Battered Women's Shelters," CFMN-CEMA, Box 44, Folder 3.

41. "History of CFLA 1977–1981," Box 1, Folder 4; and CSAC Newsletter, December 1977, Box 2, Folder—"Chicana Service Action Center," both Collection 30, CFLA-UCLA.

42. "History of Comisión Femenil de Los Angeles" CFLA-UCLA; Molina Campaign Material, CFMN-CEMA, Box 16, Folder 2. Quote is from Gloria Molina to Gloria Moreno Wycoff, June 21, 1982, CFMN-CEMA, Box 16, Folder 2.

43. John R. Chávez, *Eastside Landmark*, 189–92, 242–46.

44. Sacks, *Caring by the Hour*; Robnett, *How Long? How Long?*; Naples, *Grassroots Warriors*.

45. Examples of the CFMN and CSAC logos can be found in CFMN-CEMA, Box 2, Folder 5.

46. CSAC Newsletters, 1973–77, Box 2, Folder—"Chicana Service Action Center," Collection 30, CFLA-UCLA.

47. On the centrality of print media to the Chicano movement, see Blackwell, "Contested Histories," 59–89. Quotes are from pp. 62 and 78.

48. Viola Correa, "La Nueva Chicana," CSAC Newsletter #3, May 25, 1973, Box 2, Folder—"Chicana Service Action Center," Collection 30, CFLA-UCLA.

49. Zinn, "Gender and Ethnic Identity," 21.

50. CSAC Newsletter, vol. 4, no. 1 (1978), CFMN-CEMA, Box 44, Folder 5.

51. Anna Nieto Gomez to Chicanos in the media, March 1975, and Nieto Gomez to Flores, March 25, 1975, CFMN-CEMA, Box 38, Folder 12.

52. CSAC News Release, June 24, 1974, CFMN-CEMA, Box 38, Folder 12.

53. Flores interview; Yolanda Nava, President of CFMN, to Connie Muñoz, Chair of CSAC Board of Directors, February 5, 1975, CFMN-CEMA, Box 38, Folder 5; Anna Nieto Gomez, "Labor and Chicanas," Chicana Service Action Center pamphlet, CFMN-CEMA, Box 38, Folder 5.

54. Flores handwritten notes, "CFMN history," CFMN-CEMA, Box 9, Folder 2.

55. Flores to Project Managers, March 25, 1977, CFMN-CEMA, Box 40, Folder 5.

56. CSAC Board of Directors Report, Board of Directors Meeting Minutes, July 10, 1982, CFMN-CEMA, Box 40, Folder 9.

57. One of the messages of congratulations to CFMN was from David Lizzarga

of TELACU. Magdalena H. Beltrán, "CFMN Celebrates 20th Anniversary Gala," *La Mujer,* April 1990, 1, 3.

58. William Abeytia to Flores, July 20, 1973, Box 41, Folder 12; and Thomas Kilgore Jr. to Flores, Box 41, Folder 13, CFMN-CEMA.

59. CSAC 25th Anniversary Program, CFLA -UCLA, Part II, Box 1, CFLA-UCLA.

60. Francisca Flores Funeral Program, CFMN-CEMA, Box 24, Folder 19.

61. Orleck, *Storming Caesars Palace.*

62. Orleck, *Storming Caesar's Palace*; Greene, *Our Separate Ways*; Williams, *The Politics of Public Housing.*

Epilogue

1. *The Civil War,* film.

2. Amiri Baraka, "Speech to the Congress of African Peoples," in Vandeburg, *Modern Black Nationalism,* 149.

3. Ogbar, *Black Power,* esp. chap. 6.

4. For examples of other women's antipoverty organizations, see Orleck, *Storming Caesar's Palace*; Greene, *Our Separate Ways*; and Williams, *The Politics of Public Housing.*

5. Vaca, *The Presumed Alliance,* 85–107.

6. "Progressive City Leaders," *The Nation* (June 18, 2005), 18–19.

7. Dennis Romero, "The Rainbow Coalition," *Tu Ciudad Los Angeles,* October–November 2005, 62–71.

8. Navarro, "The Latinoization of Los Angeles," 172; and Sonenshein and Drayse, "Urban Electoral Coalitions," 570–95.

9. Sonenshein and Drayse, "Urban Electoral Coalitions"; Teresa Watanabe, "Immigration Forum Gets Intense," *LAT,* Apr. 24, 2006.

Bibliography

Manuscript Collections

California Social Welfare Archives. Specialized Libraries and Archival Collections, University of Southern California, Los Angeles.

Comisión Femenil de Los Angeles Papers. University of California, Los Angeles, Chicano Studies Research Center.

Comisión Femenil Mexicana Nacional Archives Collection. California Ethnic and Multicultural Archives. University of California, Santa Barbara. Special Collections Library.

Lyndon Baines Johnson Presidential Library, Austin, Texas.

Records of the Community Action Program, RG 381. National Archives, College Park, Maryland.

Southern California Library for Social Studies and Research, Los Angeles.

Special Collections Library. California State University, Fullerton.

Special Collections Library. California State University, Los Angeles.

Special Collections. Young Research Library, University of California, Los Angeles.

Western Regional Files. National Association for the Advancement of Colored People Collection, Library of Congress.

Government Documents

Bureau of the Census. *U.S. Census of the Population, 1950. Special Reports, Persons of Spanish Surname.* Washington, D.C.: Government Printing Office, 1953.

——. *U.S. Census of the Population, 1960. Subject Reports, Persons of Spanish Surname. Final Report PC (2)-1B.* Washington, D.C.: Government Printing Office, 1963.

California Advisory Committee to the United States Commission on Civil Rights. *Report on California: Police–Minority Group Relations in Los Angeles and the San Francisco Bay Area.* San Francisco, August 1963.

Civil Rights During the Johnson Administration, 1963–1969: A Collection from the Holdings of the Lyndon Baines Johnson Library. Frederick, Md.: University Publications of America, 1984.

Johnson, Lyndon B. *Public Papers of the Presidents, Lyndon B. Johnson.* Vol. 1. Washington, D.C.: Government Printing Office, 1963–64.

Los Angeles City Archives, Records Management Division. City Clerk's Office, Los Angeles.

Los Angeles County Board of Supervisors Records. Board of Supervisors Office, Los Angeles.

California Department of Industrial Relations, Division of Labor Statistics and Research. *Negroes and Mexican Americans in South and East Los Angeles.* San Francisco: State of California, Division of Fair Employment Practices, 1966.

Violence in the City—An End or a Beginning?: A Report by the Governor's Commission on the Los Angeles Riots, December 2, 1965.

The War on Poverty, 1964–1968: Microfilm Collection from the Lyndon Baines Johnson Library. Frederick, Md.: University Publications of America, 1986.

White House Central Files. Lyndon Baines Johnson Presidential Library. Austin, Texas, 1963–64.

Youth Opportunities Board of Greater Los Angeles. *Expanding Opportunities for Youth.* Los Angeles: Youth Opportunities Board of Greater Los Angeles, 1964.

Interviews

Collins, LeRoy. Interview by Joe B. Frantz. November 15, 1972. Transcript #AC 81-54. Lyndon Baines Johnson Library, Austin, Tex.

Flores, Francisca. Interview by Gloria Moreno-Wycoff. October 19, 1982. Box 46. CFMN-CEMA Archives, University of California, Santa Barbara Special Collections Library.

Hawkins, Augustus F. Interview by Carlos Vasquez. 1988. Transcript. UCLA Oral History Program for the California State Archives State Governmental Oral History Program.

King, Celes, III. Interview by Bruce M. Tyler and Robin D. G. Kelley. 1988. Transcript. Vol. 2. UCLA Oral History Program.

Luevano, Daniel J. Interview by Carlos Vasquez. 1988. Transcript. UCLA Oral History Program for the California State Archives State Governmental Oral History Program.

Martinez, Richard A. Interview by Carlos Vasquez. 1990. Transcript. UCLA Oral History Program for the California State Archives State Governmental Oral History Program.

Molina, Gloria. Interview by Carlos Vasquez. 1990. Transcript. UCLA Oral History Program for the California State Archives State Governmental Oral History Program.

Nava, Yolanda. Interview by Gloria Moreno-Wycoff. October 1982. CFMN-CEMA Archives, University of California, Santa Barbara Special Collections Library.

——. Interview by Michelle Moravec. January 17, 1989. The Virtual Oral/Aural History Archive (VOAHA). California State University, Long Beach. http:/// www.csulb.edu/voaha.

Sugarman, Jule M. Interview by Stephen Goodell. March 14, 1969. Transcript. Lyndon Baines Johnson Library, Austin, Texas.

Yorty, Samuel William. "Ask the Mayor." Interview by Hynda Rudd. 1987. Transcript. UCLA Oral History Program.

———. Interview by Joe B. Frantz. February 7, 1970. Transcript #AC 75-9. Lyndon Baines Johnson Library, Austin, Texas.

Books and Articles

Aaron, Henry J. *Politics and the Professors: The Great Society in Perspective.* Washington, D.C.: Brookings Institution, 1978.

Acuña, Rodolfo F. *A Community under Siege: A Chronicle of Chicanos East of the Los Angeles River 1945–1975.* Los Angeles: Chicano Studies Research Center, University of California, Los Angeles, 1984.

Allen, James P., and Eugene Turner. *The Ethnic Quilt: Population Diversity in Southern California.* Northridge, Calif.: Center for Geographical Studies, California State University, Northridge, 1997.

Ambrecht, Biliana C. S. *Politicizing the Poor: The Legacy of the War on Poverty in a Mexican-American Community.* New York: Praeger Press, 1976.

Ambrecht, Biliana C. S., and Henry P. Pacho. "Ethnic Political Mobilization in a Mexican-American Community: An Exploratory Study of East Los Angeles, 1965–1972." *Western Political Quarterly* 27, no. 3 (Sept. 1970), 500–19.

Banfield, Edward C. *Big City Politics.* New York: Random House, 1965.

Bates, Beth Tompkins. "A New Crowd Challenges the Agenda of the Old Guard in the NAACP, 1933–1941." *American Historical Review* 102 (April 1997): 340–77.

Bernstein, Irving. *Guns or Butter: The Presidency of Lyndon Johnson.* New York: Oxford University Press, 1996.

Blackwell, Maylei. "Contested Histories: *Las Hijas de Cuauhtémoc,* Chicana Feminisms, and Print Culture in the Chicano Movement, 1968–1973." In *Chicana Feminisms: A Critical Reader,* ed. Gabriela F. Arredondo et al., 59–89. Durham, N.C.: Duke University Press, 2003.

Blauner, Robert. "Whitewash over Watts: The Future of the McCone Commission Report." In *Mass Violence in America: The Los Angeles Riots,* ed. Robert M. Fogelson, 167–88. New York: Arno Press, 1969.

Bollens, John C., and Grant B. Geyer. *Yorty: Politics of a Constant Candidate.* Pacific Palisades, Calif.: Palisades Publishing, 1973.

Boyle, Kevin. *The UAW and the Heyday of American Liberalism 1945–1968.* Ithaca, N.Y.: Cornell University Press, 1995.

Branch, Taylor. *At Canaan's Edge: America in the King Years, 1965–1968.* New York: Simon and Schuster, 2006.

———. *Pillar of Fire: America in the King Years.* New York: Simon and Schuster, 1998.

Brown, Scot. *Fighting for U.S.: Maulana Karenga, the U.S. Organization, and Black Cultural Nationalism.* New York: New York University Press, 2003.

Browning, Rufus P., Dale Rogers Marshall, and David Tabb. *Protest Is Not Enough.* Berkeley: University of California Press, 1984.

Bullock, Paul. *Watts: The Aftermath.* New York: Grove Press, 1969.

———. *Youth in the Labor Market: Employment Patterns and Career Aspirations in Watts and East Los Angeles.* Los Angeles: UCLA Institute of Industrial Relations, 1972.

Califano, Joseph A. *The Triumph and Tragedy of Lyndon Johnson.* New York: Simon & Schuster, 1991.

Carmichael, Stokely, and Charles V. Hamilton. *Black Power: The Politics of Liberation in America.* New York: Random House, 1967.

Chapman, Abraham, ed. *Black Voices: An Anthology of African American Literature.* New York: New American Library, 1968.

Chávez, Ernesto. *¡Mi Raza Primero!: Nationalism, Identity, and Insurgency in the Chicano Movement in Los Angeles, 1966–1978.* Berkeley: University of California Press, 2002.

Chávez, John R. *Eastside Landmark: A History of the East Los Angeles Community Union, 1968–1993.* Palo Alto, Calif.: Stanford University Press, 1998.

Clark, Kenneth B., and Jeanette Hopkins. *A Relevant War against Poverty: A Study of Community Action Programs and Observable Social Change.* New York: Harper and Row, 1969.

Clayson, William. "'The Barrios and the Ghettos Have Organized!': Community Action, Political Acrimony and the War on Poverty in San Antonio." *Journal of Urban History* 28, no. 2 (January 2002): 158–84.

Cloward, Richard A., and Lloyd Ohlin. *Delinquency and Opportunity.* New York: Free Press, 1960.

Cohen, Jerry, and William S. Murphy. *Burn, Baby, Burn!: The Los Angeles Race Riot, August 1965.* New York: Dutton, 1966.

Cohen, Nathan E., ed. *The Los Angeles Riots: A Socio-Psychological Study.* New York: Praeger, 1970.

Coleman, Vernon. "Labor Power and Social Equality: Union Politics in a Changing Economy." *Political Science Quarterly* 103, no. 4 (Winter 1988–89): 687–705.

Conot, Robert. *Rivers of Blood, Years of Darkness: The Unforgettable Classic Account of the Watts Riot.* New York: Morrow, 1968.

Davies, Gareth. *From Opportunity to Entitlement: The Transformation and Decline of Great Society Liberalism.* Lawrence: University of Kansas Press, 1996.

———. "Understanding the War on Poverty: The Advantages of a Canadian Perspective." *Journal of Policy History* 9, no. 4 (1997): 425–49.

Davis, Mike. *City of Quartz: Excavating the Future in Los Angeles.* London: Verso Press, 1990.

Dear, Michael J., H. Erick Shockman, and Greg Hise, eds. *Rethinking Los Angeles.* Thousand Oaks, Calif.: Sage Publications, 1996.

De Graaf, Lawrence B. "The City of Black Angels: Emergence of the Los Angeles Ghetto, 1890–1930." *Pacific Historical Review* 89 (1970): 323–52.

De Graaf, Lawrence B., Kevin Mulroy, and Quintard Taylor. *Seeking El Dorado: African Americans in California*. Seattle: University of Washington Press, 2001.

"The East Los Angeles Community Union." *Community Development Corporation Oral History Project*. New York: Pratt Institute Center for Community and Environmental Development, 2000.

Escobar, Edward J. "The Dialectics of Repression: The Los Angeles Police Department and the Chicano Movement, 1968–1971." *Journal of American History* 79, no. 4 (March 1991): 1483–1514.

Espinoza, Dionne. "'Revolutionary Sisters': Women's Solidarity and Collective Identification among Chicana Brown Berets in East Los Angeles, 1967–1970." *Aztlán* 26, no. 1 (Spring 2001): 17–58.

Flamming, Douglas. *Bound for Freedom: Black Los Angeles in Jim Crow America*. Berkeley: University of California Press, 2005.

Flores, Francisca. "Comisión Femenil Mexicana." *Regeneración* 2, no. 1 (1971): 6–7.

Fogelson, Robert M. "White on Black: A Critique of the McCone Commission Report on the Los Angeles Riots." In *Mass Violence in America: The Los Angeles Riots*, ed. Robert M. Fogelson, 113–43. New York: Arno Press, 1969.

Forbes, Jack D. "The Early African Heritage of California." In *Seeking El Dorado: African Americans in California*, ed. Lawrence B. De Graaf, Kevin Mulroy, and Quintard Taylor, 73–97. Seattle: University of Washington Press, 2001.

Franklin, Grace A., and Randall B. Ripley. *CETA: Politics and Policy, 1973–1982*. Knoxville: University of Tennessee Press, 1984.

Gaines, Kevin. "Rethinking Race and Class in African-American Struggles for Equality, 1885–1941." *American Historical Review* 102 (April 1997): 378–87.

——. *Uplifting the Race: Black Leadership, Politics, and Culture in the Twentieth Century*. Chapel Hill: University of North Carolina Press, 1996.

Garcia, Alma M. "Introduction." In *Chicana Feminist Thought: The Basic Historical Writings*, ed. Alma M. Garcia, 1–16. New York: Routledge Press, 1997.

Garcia, Mario T. *Memories of Chicano History: The Life and Narrative of Bert Corona*. Berkeley: University of California Press, 1994.

Garrow, David J. *Bearing the Cross: Martin Luther King, Jr., and the Southern Christian Leadership Conference*. New York: W. Morrow, 1986.

Gerstle, Gary. *American Crucible: Race and Nation in the Twentieth Century*. Princeton, N.J.: Princeton University Press, 2001.

——. "Race and the Myth of the Liberal Consensus." *Journal of American History* 82, no. 2 (September 1985): 579–86.

Gómez-Quiñones, Juan. *Chicano Politics: Reality and Promise, 1940–1990*. Albuquerque: University of New Mexico Press, 1990.

Gonzales, Manual G. *Mexicanos: A History of Mexicans in the United States.* Bloomington: University of Indiana Press, 1999.

Gooding-Williams, Robert, ed. *Reading Rodney King: Reading Urban Uprising.* New York: Routledge Press, 1993.

Gordon, Eric. "Fortifying Community: African American History and Culture in Leimert Park." In *The Sons and Daughters of Los: Culture and Community in L.A.,* ed. David E. James, 63–84. Philadelphia: Temple University Press, 2003.

Gorman, Joseph Bruce. *Kefauver: A Political Biography.* New York: Oxford University Press, 1971.

Greene, Christina. *Our Separate Ways: Women and the Black Freedom Movement in Durham, North Carolina.* Chapel Hill: University of North Carolina Press, 2005.

Greenstone, J. David, and Paul E. Peterson. *Race and Authority in Urban Politics: Community Participation in the War on Poverty.* New York: Russell Sage Foundation, 1973.

Grossman, James. *Land of Hope: Chicago, Black Southerners and the Great Migration.* Chicago: University of Chicago Press, 1989.

Hall, Jacquelyn Dowd. "The Long Civil Rights Movement and the Political Uses of the Past." *Journal of American History* 91, no. 4 (March 2005), 1233–63.

Harrington, Michael. *The Other America.* Baltimore: Penguin Books, 1963.

Henry, Charles P. "Black-Chicano Coalitions: Possibilities and Problems." *Western Journal of Black Studies* 4, no. 4 (Winter 1980): 222–32.

Horne, Gerald. "Black Fire: 'Riot' and 'Revolt' in Los Angeles, 1965 and 1992." In *Seeking El Dorado: African Americans in California,* ed. Lawrence B. De Graaf, Kevin Mulroy, and Quintard Taylor, 377–404. Seattle: University of Washington Press, 2001.

——. *Fire This Time: The Watts Uprising and the 1960s.* Charlottesville: University of Virginia Press, 1995.

Isasi-Diaz, Ada Maria, Elena Olazagasti-Segovia et al. "Roundtable Discussion: Mujeristas: Who We Are and What We Are About." *Journal of Feminist Studies in Religion* 8, no. 1 (Spring 1992): 105–28.

Jackson, Thomas F. *From Civil Rights to Human Rights: Martin Luther King, Jr., and the Struggle for Economic Justice.* Philadelphia: University of Pennsylvania Press, 2007.

——. "The State, The Movement, and the Urban Poor: The War on Poverty and Political Mobilization in the 1960s." In *The "Underclass" Debate,* ed. Michael B. Katz, 403–39. Princeton, N.J.: Princeton University Press, 1993.

Joseph, Peniel E. *Waiting 'Til the Midnight Hour: A Narrative History of Black Power in America.* New York: Henry Holt, 2006.

——, ed. *The Black Power Movement: Rethinking the Civil Rights–Black Power Era.* New York: Routledge, 2006.

Katz, Michael B. *Improving Poor People: The Welfare State, the 'Underclass' and Urban Schools as History.* Princeton, N.J.: Princeton University Press, 1995.

——. *The Undeserving Poor: From the War on Poverty to the War on Welfare.* New York: Pantheon Books, 1989.

Kearns, Doris. *Lyndon Johnson and the American Dream.* New York: Harper & Row, 1976.

Knapp, Daniel, and Kenneth Polk. *Scouting the War on Poverty: Social Reform in the Kennedy Administration.* Lexington, Mass.: Heath/Lexington Books, 1971.

Krainz, Thomas. *Delivering Aid: Implementing Progressive Era Welfare in the American West.* Albuquerque: University of New Mexico Press, 2005.

Kramer, Ralph M. *Participation of the Poor: Comparative Cases in the War on Poverty.* Englewood Cliffs, N.J.: Prentice Hall, 1969.

Laslett, John H. M. "Historical Perspectives: Immigration and the Rise of a Distinctive Urban Region, 1900–1970." In *Ethnic Los Angeles,* ed. Roger Waldinger and Mehdi Bozorgmehr, 39–75. New York: Russell Sage Foundation, 1996.

Leonard, Kevin Allen. *The Battle for Los Angeles: Racial Ideology and World War II.* Albuquerque: University of New Mexico Press, 2006.

——. "In the Interest of All Races: African Americans and Interracial Cooperation in Los Angeles during and after World War II." In *Seeking El Dorado: African Americans in California,* ed. Lawrence B. De Graaf, Kevin Mulroy, and Quintard Taylor, 309–40. Seattle: University of Washington Press, 2001.

Lichtenstein, Nelson. *The Most Dangerous Man in Detroit: Walter Reuther and the Fate of American Labor.* New York: Basic Books, 1995.

López, Ian F. Haney. *Racism on Trial: The Chicano Fight for Justice.* Cambridge: Harvard University Press, 2003.

Marín, Marguerite V. *Social Protest in an Urban Barrio: A Study of the Chicano Movement, 1966–1974.* Lanham, Md.: University Press of America, 1991.

Mariscal, George. *Brown-Eyed Children of the Sun: Lessons from the Chicano Movement, 1965–1975.* Albuquerque: University of New Mexico Press, 2005.

——, ed. *Aztlán and Viet Nam: Chicano and Chicana Experiences of the War.* Berkeley: University of California Press, 1999.

Marquez, Benjamin. *LULAC: The Evolution of a Mexican American Political Organization.* Austin: University of Texas Press.

Marris, Peter, and Martin Rein, eds. *Dilemmas of Social Reform: Poverty and Community Action in the United States.* New York: Atherton Press, 1967.

Marshall, Dale Rogers. *The Politics of Participation in Poverty: A Case Study of the Board of the Economic and Youth Opportunities Agency of Greater Los Angeles.* Berkeley: University of California Press, 1971.

Martinez, Elizabeth Sutherland, and Enriqueta Longeaux y Vasquez. *Viva la Raza! The Struggle of the Mexican-American People.* Garden City, N.Y.: 1974.

McGirr, Lisa. *Suburban Warriors: The Origins of the New American Right*. Princeton, N.J.: Princeton University Press, 2001.

Mirandé, Alfredo, and Evangelina Enriquez. *La Chicana: The Mexican-American Woman*. Chicago: University of Chicago Press, 1979.

Moynihan, Daniel P. *Maximum Feasible Misunderstanding: Community Action in the War on Poverty*. New York: Free Press, 1969.

Naples, Nancy. *Grassroots Warriors: Activist Mothering, Community Work, and the War on Poverty*. New York: Routledge, 1995.

Navarro, Armando. "The Latinoization of Los Angeles: The Politics of Polarization." In *Multiethnic Coalition Building in Los Angeles*, ed. Eui-Young Yu and Edward T. Chang, 169–86. Claremont, Calif.: Regina Books, 1995.

Nicolaides, Becky M. *My Blue Heaven: Life and Politics in the Working-Class Suburbs of Los Angeles, 1920–1965*. Chicago: University of Chicago Press, 2002.

Nieto Gomez, Anna. "Chicana Service Action Center." In *Chicana Feminist Thought: The Basic Historical Writings*, ed. Alma M. Garcia, 148–49. New York: Routledge Press, 1997.

———. Chicanas in the Labor Force." *Encuentro Femenil* 1, no. 2 (1974): 28–33.

Nightingale, Carl Husemoller. "The Global Inner City: Toward a Historical Analysis." In *W. E. B. Du Bois, Race and the City*, ed. Michael B. Katz and Thomas J. Sugrue, 207–58. Philadelphia: University of Pennsylvania Press, 1998.

O'Connor, Alice. "Community Action, Urban Reform and the fight Against Poverty." *Journal of Urban History* 22 (July 1996): 586–625.

Ogbar, Jeffrey O. G. *Black Power: Radical Politics and African American Identity*. Baltimore: Johns Hopkins University Press, 2004.

Oliver, Melvin L., James H. Johnson, Jr., and Walter C. Farrell. "Anatomy of a Rebellion: A Political-Economic Analysis." In *Reading Rodney King: Reading Urban Uprising*, ed. Robert Gooding-Williams, 117–41. New York: Routledge Press, 1993.

Ong, Paul, and Evelyn Blumenberg. "Income and Racial Inequality in Los Angeles." In *The City: Los Angeles and Urban Theory at the End of the Twentieth Century*, ed. Allen J. Scott and Edward W. Soja, 311–35. Berkeley: University of California Press, 1996.

Orleck, Annelise. *Storming Caesar's Palace: How Black Mothers Fought Their Own War on Poverty*. Boston: Beacon Press, 2005.

Oropeza, Lorena. ¡*Raza Sí! ¡Guerra No!: Chicano Protest and Patriotism during the Viet Nam War Era*. Berkeley: University of California Press, 2005.

Ortiz, Isidro D. "Chicano Urban Politics and the Politics of Reform in the Seventies." *Western Political Quarterly* 37, no. 4 (December 1984): 564–77.

Patterson, James T. *America's Struggle against Poverty: 1900–1980*. Cambridge: Harvard University Press, 1981.

Payne, J. Gregory, and Scot C. Ratzan. *Tom Bradley: The Impossible Dream*. Santa Monica, Calif.: Roundtable Publishing, 1986.

Pettigrew, Thomas F. *Tom Bradley's Campaigns for Governor: The Dilemma of Race and Political Strategies.* Washington, D.C.: Joint Center for Political Studies, 1988.

Pitt, Leonard, and Dale Pitt. *Los Angeles A to Z: An Encyclopedia of the City and County.* Berkeley: University of California Press, 1997.

Piven, Frances Fox, and Richard A. Cloward. *Regulating the Poor: The Functions of Public Welfare.* New York: Random House, 1971.

Pulido, Laura. *Black, Brown, Yellow, and Left: Radical Activism in Los Angeles.* Berkeley: University of California Press, 2006.

Pycior, Julie Leininger. *LBJ and Mexican Americans: The Paradox of Power.* Austin: University of Texas Press, 1997.

Quadagno, Jill S. *The Color of Welfare: How Racism Undermined the War on Poverty.* New York: Oxford University Press, 1994.

Ralph, James R., Jr. *Northern Protest: Martin Luther King, Jr., Chicago, and the Civil Rights Movement.* Cambridge: Harvard University Press, 1993.

Robnett, Belinda. *How Long? How Long?: African-American Women in the Struggle for Civil Rights.* New York: Oxford University Press, 1997.

Rocco, Raymond. "Latino Los Angeles: Reframing Boundaries/Borders." In *The City: Los Angeles and Urban Theory at the End of the Twentieth Century,* ed. Allen J. Scott and Edward W. Soja, 365–89. Berkeley: University of California Press, 1996.

Rojas, James. "The Cultural Landscape of a Latino Community." In *Landscape and Race in the United States,* ed. Richard H. Schein, 177–85. New York: Routledge Press, 2006.

Romo, Ricardo. *East Los Angeles: History of a Barrio.* Austin: University of Texas Press, 1983.

Rorabaugh, W. J. *Berkeley at War: The 1960s.* New York: Oxford University Press, 1989.

Ruiz, Vicki L. *From Out of the Shadows: Mexican Women in Twentieth Century America.* New York: Oxford University Press, 1998.

Russell, Judith. *Economics, Bureaucracy, and Race: How Keynesians Misguided the War on Poverty.* New York: Columbia University Press, 2004.

Sacks, Karen Brodkin. *Caring by the Hour: Women, Work, and Organizing at Duke Medical Center.* Champaign: University of Illinois Press, 1988.

Sánchez, George J. *Becoming Mexican American: Ethnicity, Culture and Identity in Chicano Los Angeles, 1900–1945.* New York: Oxford University Press, 1993.

Scoble, Harry M. "Negro Politics in Los Angeles: The Quest for Power." In *The Los Angeles Riots: A Socio-Psychological Study,* 638–75. New York: Praeger, 1970.

Scott, Allen J., and Edward W. Soja, eds. *The City: Los Angeles and Urban Theory at the End of the Twentieth Century.* Berkeley: University of California Press, 1996.

Scudder, Kenyon J., and Kenneth S. Beam. *The Twenty Billion Dollar Challenge: A National Program for Delinquency Prevention.* New York: Putnam, 1961.

Sears, David O. "Political Attitudes of Los Angeles Negroes." In *The Los Angeles Riots: A Socio-Psychological Study,* ed. Nathan E. Cohen, 676–705. New York: Praeger, 1970.

Sears, David O., and John B. McConahay. "The Politics of Discontent." In *The Los Angeles Riots: A Socio-Psychological Study,* ed. Nathan E. Cohen, 413–79. New York: Praeger, 1970.

Self, Robert O. *American Babylon: Race and the Struggle for Postwar Oakland.* Princeton, N.J.: Princeton University Press, 2003.

Sides, Josh. *L.A. City Limits: African American Los Angeles from the Great Depression to the Present.* Berkeley: University of California Press, 2003.

——. "Rethinking Black Migration: A Perspective from the West." In *Moving Stories: Migration and the American West 1850–2000,* ed. Scott E. Caspar and Lucinda M. Long, 190–210. Reno: Nevada Humanities Commission, 2001.

Sonenshein, Raphael J. *Politics in Black and White: Race and Power in Los Angeles.* Princeton, N.J.: Princeton University Press, 1993.

Sonenshein, Raphael J., and Mark H. Drayse. "Urban Electoral Coalitions in an Age of Immigration: Time and Place in the 2001 and 2005 Los Angeles Mayoral Primaries." *Political Geography* 25, no. (June 2005), 570–95.

Sugrue, Thomas J. *The Origins of the Urban Crisis: Race and Inequality in Postwar Detroit.* Princeton, N.J.: Princeton University Press, 1996.

——. "The Structure of Urban Poverty: The Reorganization of Space and Work in Three Periods of American History." In *The Underclass Debate: Views from History,* ed. Michael B. Katz, 85–117. Princeton, N.J.: Princeton University Press, 1993.

Taylor, Quintard. *The Forging of a Black Community: Seattle's Central District from 1870 through the Civil Rights Era.* Seattle: University of Washington Press, 1994.

——. *In Search of the Racial Frontier: African Americans in the American West, 1528–1990.* New York: W. W. Norton, 1998.

Tyler, Bruce M. "The Rise and Decline of the Watts Summer Festival, 1965 to 1986," *American Studies* 31, no. 2 (1990): 63–66.

Unger, Irwin. *The Best of Intentions: The Triumphs and Failures of the Great Society under Kennedy, Johnson, and Nixon.* New York: Doubleday, 1996.

Vaca, Nicolás C. *The Presumed Alliance: The Unspoken Conflict between Latinos and Blacks and What It Means for America.* N.Y.: HarperCollins, 2004

Van DeBurg, William L. *Modern Black Nationalism: From Marcus Garvey to Louis Farrakhan.* New York: New York University Press, 1997.

——. *New Day in Babylon: The Black Power Movement and American Culture, 1965–1975.* Chicago: University of Chicago Press, 1992.

Viorst, Milton. *Fire in the Streets: America in the 1960s.* New York: Simon & Schuster, 1979.

Weisbrot, Robert. *Freedom Bound: A History of America's Civil Rights Movement.* New York: Penguin Books, 1991.

Whitaker, Matthew C. *Race Work: The Rise of Civil Rights in the Urban West.* Lincoln: University of Nebraska Press, 2005.

White, Richard. "Race Relations in the American West." *American Quarterly* 38, no. 3 (1986): 396–416.

Wiese, Andrew. *Places of Their Own: African American Suburbanization in the Twentieth Century.* Chicago: University of Chicago Press, 2004.

Wild, Mark. *Street Meeting: Multiethnic Neighborhoods in Early Twentieth-Century Los Angeles.* Berkeley: University of California Press, 2005.

Williams, Rhonda Y. *The Politics of Public Housing: Black Women's Struggles Against Urban Inequality.* New York: Oxford University Press, 2004.

Wilson, William Julius. *The Truly Disadvantaged: The Inner City, the Underclass, and Public Policy.* Chicago: University of Chicago Press, 1987.

——. *When Work Disappears: The World of the New Urban Poor.* New York: Knopf, 1996.

Yu, Eui-Young, and Edward T. Chang, eds. *Multiethnic Coalition Building in Los Angeles.* Claremont, Calif.: Regina Books, 1995.

Zinn, Maxine Baca. "Gender and Ethnic Identity among Chicanas." In *Chicana Leadership: The Frontiers Reader,* ed. Yolanda Flores Niemann, with Susan Armitage, Patricia Hart, and Karen Weatherman, 15–29. Lincoln: University of Nebraska Press, 2002.

Newspapers

The Los Angeles Herald Examiner
The Los Angeles Sentinel
The Los Angeles Times

Theses and Dissertations

Bauman, Robert. "Race, Class and Political Power: The Implementation of the War on Poverty in Los Angeles." Ph.D. diss., University of California, Santa Barbara, 1998.

——. "From Tuberculosis Sanatorium to Medical Center: The History of Olive View Medical Center, 1920–1989." Master's thesis, University of California, Santa Barbara, 1989.

Glasgow, Douglas Graham. "The Sons of Watts Improvement Association: Analysis of Mobility Aspirations and Life-Styles in the Aftermath of the Watts Riot, 1965." Ph.D. diss., University of Southern California, 1968.

Kurashige, Scott Tadao. "Transforming Los Angeles: Black and Japanese American Struggles for Racial Equality in the 20th Century." Ph.D. diss., University of California, Los Angeles, 2000.

Tyler, Bruce Michael. "Black Radicalism in Southern California, 1950–1982." Ph.D. diss., University of California, Los Angeles, 1983.

Documentaries

CBS Reports: Watts, Riot or Revolt. Prod., Jack Beck. Originally aired December 7, 1965. New York: Films for the Humanities and Sciences, 2000.

The Civil War. A Florentine Films Production. Exec. prod., Ken Burns. New York: PBS Video, 1990.

Index